PLANNING
for
NONPLANNERS

DARRYL J. ELLIS • PETER P. PEKAR, Jr.

PLANNING
for
NONPLANNERS

Planning Basics for Managers

In cooperation with
the North American Society
for Corporate Planning

**A Division of
American Management Associations**

Library of Congress Cataloging in Publication Data
Ellis, Darryl J
    Planning for nonplanners.

    Bibliography: p.
    Includes index.
    1. Corporate planning.   I. Pekar, Peter P., joint
author.   II. North American Society for Corporate
Planning.   III. Title.
HD30.28.E44   658.4'01   80-66865
    ISBN 0-8144-5593-X

© 1980 AMACOM
A division of American Management Associations, New York.
All rights reserved. Printed in the United States of America.

First Printing

Acknowledgments

It is not possible to acknowledge all those friends and business acquaintances who have furnished ideas and materials for this book, but we must record our debt to Malcolm Pennington, president of the Marketing and Planning Group, whose acute observations and original theories have been a constant stimulus and who gave his precious time, encouragement, and valuable suggestions. Finally we would both like to thank our families for their patience under many trials. Without their support, this work could not have been completed.

Darryl J. Ellis
Peter P. Pekar, Jr.

Contents

	Introduction: The Need	1
1	The Evolution and the Individual	4
2	Planning: A Necessity or a Luxury?	14
3	Planning—Business Style (Part 1)	31
4	Planning—Business Style (Part 2)	91
5	Looking Ahead: Thinking Globally, Acting Locally	133
	Bibliography	147
	Index	149

Introduction:
THE NEED

My interest is in the future because I am going to spend the rest of my life there. —CHARLES F. KETTERING

The world has never appeared as hostile, bewildering, or unstable as it does today. Yet everyone wants to formulate concrete plans for the future. The problem is that often these plans focus on numbers rather than on the strategic issues that are the key to success of an organization.

One need only review the national cancer program to uncover a perfect example of this type of nonthinking. With considerable fanfare and ballyhoo, President Nixon assured us that if we would spend $40 billion over 20 years on medical research, a cure for cancer would be found. Why is it generally believed that we can do this? Well, didn't we put a man on the moon in nine years? Didn't we build the Panama Canal when everyone else failed? Weren't we responsible for harnessing nuclear power in four short years? And, after all, are we not the greatest nation on earth for getting things done?

Let no one forget what the historian H. G. Wells told us: "Ignorance is the first penalty of pride." Despite the medical profession's doubts and lack of knowledge, the spending has gone on. What have we found? Unlike previous national programs, which focused on the attainment of a single goal, cancer is a multifaceted problem that does not lend itself to a one-dimensional solution.

Does this sound familiar? How many times are you asked to generate a simple solution to a multifaceted problem? The reason we have written this book is that we have found too many business plans that throw dollars at (or withhold dollars from) problems in the hope that they will go away. Seldom are the strategic issues addressed. Regardless of what they say—and most managers *talk* planning—they don't believe in planning.

We recently attended a seminar in which a man we know intimately was to speak on planning. He is the chief executive of a company that formerly ranked among the Dow Jones 30 Industrials. We attended because we couldn't understand what he could contribute. We know he has spent a million dollars or more in developing a planning system. Not only was a numerical data base implemented, but the CEO also received, in his words, the ultimate planning tool—"a war room." However, planning at this company seldom contributes to corporate decisions, and goal setting remains weak in the corporate hierarchy today.

What this CEO failed to realize is that all he has done with these elaborate procedures is to computerize the budgeting process. All planning at this company focuses on numbers and not on strategic issues. Why? Although the system was modernized, the philosophy never changed. He still holds to the opinion that planning is an extension of the budgeting process. But this is the exact opposite of how it should be: good planning identifies the key issues to which numbers can later be attached.

In this book, we attempt to present guidelines for managers who need to plan, but are unfamiliar with planning concepts. It is our intent that after reading this book and using it as a tool, you will have taken the first step toward creating and using a strategic planning system in your business. Bear in mind that strategic

Table 1. Time period from conception to realization of major inno-
vations.

	Conception	Realization	Incubation Interval
Antibiotics	1910	1940	30 years
Automatic transmission	1930	1946	16 years
Ball-point pen	1938	1945	7 years
Cellophane	1900	1912	12 years
Dry soup mixes	1943	1962	19 years
Frozen foods	1908	1923	15 years
Heart pacemaker	1928	1960	32 years
Hybrid corn	1908	1933	25 years
Instant coffee	1934	1956	22 years
Liquid shampoo	1950	1958	8 years
Nuclear energy	1919	1965	46 years
Nylon	1927	1939	12 years
Photography	1782	1838	56 years
Radar	1904	1939	35 years
Roll-on deodorant	1948	1955	7 years
Self-winding wristwatch	1923	1939	16 years
Television	1884	1947	63 years
Video tape recorder	1950	1956	6 years
Xerox copying	1935	1950	15 years
Zipper	1883	1913	30 years

SOURCE: Stephen Rosen, *Future Facts*. New York: Simon & Schuster, 1976.

thinking encompasses a vast panorama of ideas and occurrences that should act as a guide for the future.

Many products that are in common use today appear to have had a simple development. But think for a moment about some of the important items we now take for granted. Today the time cycle for innovation has not shortened, but the life cycle for products has shortened dramatically. Accelerating change has increased pressures for successful innovation. To survive and prosper in this environment requires a commitment to strategic thinking and planning.

1

THE EVOLUTION
AND
THE INDIVIDUAL

THE EVOLUTION

The wise man's eyes are in his head, but the fool walketh in darkness.
——ECCLESIASTES, ii:14

We tend to think we are the most advanced and sophisticated society that has yet inhabited the earth. Everyone says we can no longer evolve haphazardly; we must plan our future. Is this so very different from the past?

Contrary to popular belief, planning is not a new phenomenon. Turn to the first page of the Bible. Jehovah used a six-day planned action program to create the earth (and only He knows how long it took to do the universe). His plan was one of elegant simplicity. Man did not come about until all the elements necessary for his survival were in place. It is worthwhile to remember this example in your planning. Everything must follow a simple and logical sequence of events.

A Roman Failure

Through the ages, man has attempted to follow this approach with varying degrees of success. Consider the Roman Empire, which lasted more than a thousand years—a good deal longer than most of our modern nation-states. Historians are of the opinion that Rome's decline and fall can be attributed to a multitude of maladies—moral decay, political instability, religious turmoil, and complacency. We think that these are all symptoms. We believe Rome fell because of a lack of strategic foresight. Within her organizational and governmental framework, she had built a culture that was Greek in origin, but Roman in application and result. Even in all her splendor, she made no advance in science and no mechanical improvements.[1] For example, 400 years before the time of the emperor Pious Antonious (161 A.D.), Hero of Alexandria made the first steam engine.[2] (This was during Greece's halcyon days.) Such beginnings of science were among the neglected treasures later uncovered by historians.

Despite Rome's renown for military prowess, nothing was done to improve tactics or weapons for over 200 years. The Romans learned nothing from the disaster experienced at Carrhae (53 B.C.) when the Parthians, using mounted archers and mounted lancers, applied a hit-and-run Panzer-type warfare, quite modern in concept, and killed or captured more than 30,000 Romans. Two hundred years after this defeat, the Romans continued to wage war, using identical tactics against the highly mobile nomads of Asia who easily outflanked them and decimated them with mounted archers.

What can you as a manager learn from Rome's experience? Although you might find yourself in a strong or dominant market

[1] Will Durant, *Caesar and Christ* (New York: Simon & Schuster, 1944).
[2] H. G. Wells, *The Outline of History* (New York: Doubleday, 1971).

position, *don't assume that the status quo will continue!* Management must continue to seek out strategic advice and act accordingly, or in time your business may be outflanked. Henry Ford held a dominant position in the automobile industry with a highly successful product, the Model T. But he refused to consider a new model or even a new color. ("Paint them any color you please so long as it is black.") This allowed competitors to enter the market and establish strong positions with different models and colors that appealed to different market segments.

The Age of Christianity

A phoenix arose from the ashes of Rome's failure, the first multinational service organization—the Catholic Church. Starting with no market share, but a good idea, it has outlasted the Roman Empire by a thousand years while at the same time extending its influence further than the Empire itself. Let's look at the strategic plan the Church used. Starting in Judea with limited distribution capabilities and a hostile market environment, the Church transported its ideas to a more receptive market. The Emperor Constantine, recognizing symptoms of Rome's decay, strengthened himself through a merger with the Church to provide a unifying force. At the battle of Milvan Bridge (312 A.D.), he placed the Church's monogram upon the shields and banners of his armies. Constantine's tactic raised morale and, though he was heavily outnumbered, he was victorious. The Church was now an equal.

From this base, the Church extended its market penetration by adapting itself to local conditions, incorporating features of other religions (products) into those of its own, and using market strength to dominate competitors.

By the Council of Nicea in 325 A.D., when the organization of the Church was firmly established, it had essentially 100 percent of its potential religious market. Management quickly decided to move into a new product area, politics. Competition was keen, but the Church had a strong organization, capable, well-trained executives, and ample funds. It soon became a significant factor in the market. The high point came in 1177 when the Holy Roman Emperor, Frederick Barbarossa, was compelled to kiss the feet of the Pope to demonstrate the Pope's supremacy.

However, the Church was unable to achieve dominance of the political market. Centuries of having a 100 percent share of its basic market had resulted in a stratified, bureaucratic, inflexible organization. Pope Urban II was concerned about both his organization and a declining position in the political market when he decided to open a new geographic market in 1095 by starting the Crusades. Unfortunately, this major strategic decision was made with almost no market research. The Moslems had better than a 90 percent share of the religious market in the Near East, they were well organized and well financed, and possessed a younger and more agile organization. The Church was unable to carve out a market position of any significance.

Worse, the Crusades brought unexpected competition in the home market, not from the Islamic religion, but from the ideas that the Crusaders brought back with them. In general, the discovery by the Crusaders that adherents of another faith could be civilized, humane, and trustworthy contributed to the weakening of orthodox Christian belief. (Another major effect of the Crusades was the introduction to Europe of Middle Eastern commerce and industry, along with the expansion of geographic knowledge.) This led to a questioning of the structure, administration, and strategic goals of the Church from its own executives. Because it was bureaucratic and inflexible, the Church was unable to provide opportunities for innovators within its structure. As a result, its own executives (starting with Martin Luther and his 95 Theses in 1517) departed to form their own competing enterprises.

The entrepreneurs have been notably successful. The Catholic

Church is down to perhaps 30 percent market share where it formerly dominated, and brand loyalty has weakened steadily. Nevertheless, the Church is still the market leader, and is the longest lasting and most successful organization in history. Its management is currently engaged in a lengthy reassessment of goals and strategies to meet the requirements of a new environment. Today, after many years of neglect, the Church is attempting to revitalize its product and regain its former dominant position.

What Is the Lesson?

What can managers of other enterprises learn from this example? Markets and environments are constantly changing; businesses must be dynamic and flexible to keep up; and it is folly to attempt to penetrate new markets without thorough environmental research.

Consider our own country, the United States, probably the most powerful country the world has ever known. Never has such a small number of people been so successful in extending its influence so far. With 6 percent of the world's population, we account for about 40 percent of the production of the non-Communist world and we outproduce the total of all Communist countries. No point on the globe is outside the reach of our weapons, and we have the potential to annihilate all life on this planet. Yet it has been said, "the American Empire came into being without the intentions or knowledge of the American people."[3] How has the U.S. achieved this great influence? The consumer spirit has forged American foreign policy without the overt intention of exploitation, a policy much different from those adopted by the more traditional colonial powers.

Was this America's "grand plan"? Not really. Fortunately for the U.S., at critical times some of our decision makers had strategic

---

[3] Claude Julien, *America's Empire* (New York: Pantheon, 1971).

foresight. Some examples which immediately come to mind are Thomas Jefferson and the purchase of the Louisiana Territory; President James Monroe and the doctrine of American self-determination; and Secretary of State William Seward and the purchase of Alaska.

However, the United States has at times toyed with the concept of planning. Prior to 1900, three notable examples stand out: the mapping of the Northwest Territory; the building of the Erie Canal; and the construction of a linked, cross-continental railroad system.

In this century, we have seen additional attempts to use planning, such as the Panama Canal, the Tennessee Valley Authority, the Manhattan Project (to build the first atomic bomb), and the NASA space program.

What is the unifying thread of all these programs? They have all had single purposes, have been relatively short in duration, and are uniquely different from other daily affairs. But the world was simpler then. America was rich enough to allocate resources to nearly everything. How can a businessman forget the "halycon days" of the 1945–1970 period? Opportunity and growth appeared to be unlimited. In restrospect, even business slowdowns seemed to be beneficial, since they provided an opportunity for managers to regroup and revitalize.

Today, the picture is somewhat different. In today's environment, uncertainty is the norm. Nevertheless, we feel that industry stands at the threshold of a new era. Despite the multitude of problems, opportunities and promise are unparalleled. Through anticipated technological achievements, we could be on the verge of another "golden era." However, the road to reward will be tough. Only those with strategic foresight and superior planning will be able to reap the benefits. Dreams must be channeled into actions. And, as the historical record makes clear, planning is a necessary ingredient for survival.

Today's corporate planning systems can trace their heritage directly to those systems the U.S. government initiated during World War II, and to the space program. Using this as a base, progressive companies that acted as contractors for the government modified, adapted, and introduced planning into their corporate environments. As John W. Gardner has said, "We are all continually faced with a series of great opportunities disguised as unsolvable problems." The purpose of corporate planning is to help identify these problems and opportunities.

THE INDIVIDUAL

In good speaking, should not the mind of the speaker know the truth of the matter about which he is to speak?   —PLATO

Today, planners for the most part seem to be mired in the budgeting process. This is not strategic thinking, but merely bean counting. If what you want is that which fills out the forms and has numbers attached, we hope to change your attitude.

To plan successfully, a business needs a strategic thinker at its helm and an environment in which strategic thinking permeates all endeavors. Forget about line and staff relationships; everyone from the CEO down must adopt a planning philosophy.

What are the characteristics desirable in a successful strategic thinker? Good planning must be done by everyone, but led by exceptional people. Some characteristics which can help identify these planning leaders are:

1. *Inquisitive.* An active learner, who is insatiably curious about his business, industry in general, and the world around him, he takes the initiative to get at causative factors and reasons why. He is an avid questioner and listener, with a quick, wide-ranging mind.

2. *Conceptually uninhibited.* Imaginative, bold, and nonconformist in thinking, he looks for new ideas or new ways to apply old ones and has the intellectual power to grasp and sort implications and concepts quickly. He speaks his mind but reacts well to others' ideas.

3. *Constructively competitive.* He enjoys intellectual competition and matching wits, is adroit in verbal interplay, and is even purposefully argumentative on occasion to test the strength of others' positions. He traps others in fallacious reasoning, looks for strength and weakness in ideas, and wins debates without alienating people.

4. *Practical.* Sound, astute, and realistic in risk-balancing judgments, he is analytical and objective about what can be done, how fast, and with what resources. He avoids self-delusion, and tempers his own enthusiasms with pragmatism. His logic and manner are persuasive.

5. *Tenaciously tolerant.* He is able to cope with criticism and rejection. He realizes that people are slow to change, but attempts to persevere through the use of logic and reason.

6. *Multidisciplined.* He is knowledgeable about many disciplines, and keeps up with developments in many related fields.

Individuals like these don't grow on trees, and you should recognize that people of this nature are sometimes difficult to accept. Managers should not feel threatened by their challenges, for they provide a catalyst to stimulate creative thinking.

Ideally the planning leader will be the senior manager of the organization. But often, the top manager will need a staff planner to fill this role. Not all managers tolerate planners easily, whether they are in staff or line positions.

We know of a situation in which a parent company found it necessary to reorganize a division that operated in an environment alien to the parent company's core business. The first step in the process was to transfer from the parent company's planning staff the most able, imaginative, and thorough planner available to assist the new division general manager, who was brought in from an outside company that competed in this high-growth area. Top management felt that this would ensure the success of the new general manager in line with specified corporate objectives.

But the parent managers did not realize that, despite the new general manager's past successes, he was unfamiliar with rigorous and formal planning. His main strength had been growth through acquisition, which was neither what this business needed nor in line with the firm's objectives. The planner informed the new general manager that acquisitions could only come about after proven results. This led to a conflict, and the general manager refused to listen to the realities of the situation. As a result, he devised a scheme to promote the planner and bring in a former associate who agreed with his views. Today, the business is still faltering, and no acquisitions have been made.

Remember, as Euripides said, "It is wise even in adversity to listen to reason."

STRATEGIC RISK AND MANAGEMENT STRUCTURE

Certain risks are part of any venture. For example, offshore drilling involves greater risks than does the retail liquor business. The past predictability of performance of each business area is a convenient guidepost to the proposed strategies and results. But some knowledge of the odds against success is essential to understanding where to place money and people. For instance, in a young business the general manager usually should have the characteristics of an entrepreneur, while in a growth business, the manager should be more of a market manager. A mature industry calls for a controller-type administration.

Communication should be more informal and personal in a new business than in a mature business where a formal and more uniform type of communication is appropriate. Procedures in the former should be few and flexible; in the latter, many and structured. If management is not aware of, or is blind to, the strategy risks and managerial styles necessary to operate on the appropriate product cycle, then the predictability and profit performance indicated by strategic plans will be marred.

2

PLANNING: A Necessity or a Luxury?

BENEFITS AND THE BOTTOM LINE

The future is only a glimmer in the mind of most businesses. . . .
Executives tend to think in rather parochial terms.
                              —LAWRENCE LAVENGOOD
                              Professor of Business Policy
                              Northwestern University

Economic performance, of course, is the first and foremost purpose of a business enterprise. The effectiveness of operating performance determines the ability of the enterprise to survive, to attract suppliers of funds, and to reward the suppliers adequately. However, because they focus on this perspective, too many managers continue to allow the future to arrive day by day, and remain unconcerned about controlling the events or the time schedule. Many managers continue to be reactive and not proactive. Their actions are shaped by events. We want to persuade you not to let short-term success, profitability, or problems conceal the need for long-term strategic thinking.

The Penn Central Never Left the Station

Business history is filled with sad stories of companies who concentrated on day-to-day profit performance and neglected to perceive the hazards ahead, which eventually threatened their survival. An obvious case in point in which the industry leader led many secondary companies to the brink of disaster is that of the Penn Central. At the beginning of the twentieth century, railroads had little or no competition. Having built a cross-country distribution network during the previous 50 years, and with no perceived alternative form of competition on the horizon, they established themselves in a dominant position in the transportation industry of the United States.

Because of a lack of perspective on their marketplace, little or no foresight, and management inbreeding, it was inconceivable to railroad management that another transportation system could displace the railroad. Lacking strategic thinking, railroad management failed to develop complementary forms of transportation (such as trucking, air freight, and shipping) despite the fact that, at the time, railroads were in the best market position to do so. Within 30 years, the seeds of the railroads' demise had begun to bear fruit. Today, one need only review the history of the Penn Central collapse and the financial disaster of most of the remaining railroad competitors to comprehend the significance of this strategic error.

A&P Falls Behind

Another example of a dominant market competitor experiencing a precipitate decline is the Great Atlantic & Pacific Tea Co., Inc. (A&P). For years, A&P was the dominant force in the retail food industry. Its success was based on establishing numerous small retail outlets serving individual communities in the major markets across the United States. This strategy was appropriate when the cities of the United States were composed of loose federations of local communities, centered on an economic hub. However, A&P failed to recognize the change in the market environment in the post-World War II era. During this period, population mobility and suburban exodus accelerated.

Because individual store profitability was measured on an interim basis (annually), A&P failed to recognize either the change in its customer demographics or its weakening position in the marketplace. Within 20 years, A&P's survival was in question. Faced with obsolete and now unprofitable stores, limited access to suburban markets, the changing demographics of its store locations, and the diminished economic power of its customer base, A&P is no longer the dominant market force.

Sears Forgot Its Strength

There have been many companies that focused on short-term profitability, neglected their strategic thinking, and fell victim to short-term difficulties. Some were able to reverse this course. Perhaps the best example is Sears, Roebuck and Co. Sears traditionally measured performance on the basis of the profitability of individual stores and managers. This led to bottom-line management on a weekly basis.

During the 1950s and 1960s (a period of rapid economic growth), a strategy based on increasing profitability was easy to attain. Obvious tactics called for raising prices (thus increasing margins), emphasizing upgraded and higher quality lines, and accenting private-label merchandise which carried a higher markup. Although higher prices meant surrendering to discounters entire market segments of lower priced merchandise, the Sears strategy of "Trade Up America" worked fine, and bottom-line profits soared.

However, the historical record demonstrates that economic expansions are followed by periods of contraction. Sears and many other consumer-oriented companies ignored early warning signs. For example, per capita disposable personal income (converted to real dollars) kept moving upward from 1940 to 1972 almost without hesitation, but in the fourth quarter of 1973 it started to move steadily downward: the historic age of continuous affluence and rise in the standard of living for the United States ended in September 1973, shortly before the Arab oil embargo of the U.S.[1]

Not recognizing this change, Sears continued upgrading and, while customers' pocketbooks became pinched and their loyalty weakened, Sears kept increasing its inventories. In September 1974, a full year after the beginning of the standard-of-living decline, Sears projected a highly optimistic rebound in the fourth quarter. But as growth slackened and then turned down, it became more difficult for managers to increase profits, and they had large inventories to work off. As things turned out, 1974 profits slumped for the first time in 13 years. Because of economic conditions, customers sought lower priced merchandise from such suppliers as K Mart, J. C. Penney, and Montgomery Ward.

Recognizing its error, Sears once again focused its attention on customer desires. It has started to reemphasize its lower cost lines, to pare inventories (often with sales at sharply reduced prices), and to abandon its upgrading efforts. Of course, profits remain important. However, Sears now recognizes that short-term success should not be the only performance measure.

The Japanese Experience

We agree with Steiner[2] that comprehensive corporate planning is an exercise that helps a manager foresee new opportunities, and then permits him to use his innovative skills in exploiting them.

[1] Michael J. Kami, "Planning and Planners in the Age of Discontinuity," *Planning Review,* March 1976.

[2] George A. Steiner, *Top Management Planning* (New York: Macmillan, 1969), p. 69.

We believe that the results of good planning will be demonstrated in bottom-line performance. Because of the complexity of the business environment, most senior executives have begun to recognize planning's contribution, not only to the future of the company but to near-term profitability as well.

Perhaps this can best be understood by looking at the business thinking of managements of one of the two greatest economic competitors that the United States faces. In a recent interview, several influential Japanese managers attempted to explain their country's remarkable economic performance. Highlighted was the Japanese commitment to long-range planning:

> In Japan, we tend to think of a business as something that really should go on regardless of short-term performance—not as something to be thrown away or shut down because of fundamental assumption that the business will go on. If I fail, somebody will take over from there. We learned a great deal about systematic long-range planning from American business, yet we often feel that in the management of business, the Japanese have a longer-term orientation than Americans have.
>
> YOTARO KOBAYSHI
> *Executive Vice President*
> *Fuji Xerox*

> People are not judged on performance during a short period of time—under pressure, say, to produce an increase in earnings. They are under pressure to produce, but not in terms of the next year or two. Executives can take a longer perspective in guiding the organization, which is considered perpetual.
>
> TOSHIO OZEKI
> *Senior Manager*
> *International Divisions*
> *Nikko Securities*

Why have the Japanese been so successful in the American marketplace? To some degree, their success could not have been possible without the unintentional cooperation of their American competitors. For most of the post-World War II period, Japanese industry was primarily an industrial follower rather than an innovator, dependent upon licensing arrangements for technology. But this set of circumstances was in line with the Japanese long-range strategy. This long-range strategy was based on a four-step approach:

1. First and foremost, obtain the competitor's (often American) technology.

2. Next, protect the Japanese domestic market during its growth and consolidation phase. This was accomplished through import quotas, high tariffs, and other restrictions on foreign competitors and their products.

3. Then, reduce unit costs and gain production experience. This was achieved by penetration of markets in developing nations often overlooked by competitors.

4. Finally, after significant experience had been obtained in production, distribution, marketing, and in a thorough understanding of non-Japanese markets, they moved into the U.S. market. This move into the American marketplace was not focused on the immediate generation of profits; the strategy was to gain market share.

As the Japanese moved into the U.S. markets, they chose to compete on price, particularly in the lower ends of the marketplace. Had American manufacturers perceived the Japanese strategy, it would have been simple to counteract this thrust by shaving profit margins in the short term. However, since most American managements are measured in the short term (by both shareholders and the stock market), they were loathe to compete with the Japanese on price, and thus withdrew from the lower end of the market. Never did American management realize that once the Japanese had gained a foothold in the lower end of the marketplace, they gained customer recognition, acceptance, and a distribution network that provided a springboard from which to vault into the upper end of the marketplace.

Consider the consumer electronics business (radios, televisions, tape recorders, and calculators). U.S. manufacturers of these consumer products abandoned to the Japanese the production of low-end products, such as transistor radios and tape recorders. From this base, the Japanese manufacturers quickly moved to black-and-white and then to color television sets. As American manufacturers suffered short-term profit problems, R&D budgets were reduced, thus allowing the Japanese manufacturers to become the technological innovators. For the last few years, the standard of excellence in television has been the Sony Trinitron. But recently, Sony has fallen into the same trap as its American predecessors did—a failure to invest and develop continuous advances in technology. This has allowed U.S. manufacturers to catch up again.

This example has been repeated in numerous other product areas such as automobiles, textiles, motorcycles, steel, and cameras. By concentrating on the long-term strategic plan and accepting reduced short-term profit margins, the Japanese obtained a position of market-segment dominance, thus ensuring profitability over the long term.

AMERICAN COMPANIES THAT PRACTICE LONG-RANGE STRATEGIC PLANNING

However, some leaders of American industry have recognized that profits can be assured in the short run from good, long-range strategic thinking. Two examples come immediately to mind—General Motors and K Mart.

Even before the oil embargo of 1973–1974 highlighted the forthcoming energy crisis, General Motors had evaluated its line of vehicles and determined that on a worldwide scale, its offerings were both too heavy and too large. Thus, in the summer of 1973,

GM Engineering presented to management the first weight reduction program based on a redirection of its product lines. GM viewed the coming threat of an energy crisis as a challenge both to its dominant position in the industry and to its entire marketing strategy. Management viewed this change in the marketing environment as a menace to its survival, and called for a clean break with the previous corporate strategy (trading up) developed by Alfred Sloan during the 1920s. Sloan catapulted GM into market dominance by taking an approach to the market totally different from that of Ford. While Ford was pioneering the small car market (in the 1920s), GM captured the marketplace by concentrating on large, stylish autos.

GM management recognized that the environment of the 1970s and 1980s dictated the need for a new strategy. Management perceived that government regulations covering safety, emission control, and fuel economy, along with ever-present inflation, would throw the marketplace into turmoil. Confronted by this perceived threat to its most profitable business, management searched for a new strategy.

GM perceived that its customers were interested in comfort, performance, styling, and economy—all encompassed in a smaller package. GM's first line of defense was to take the offense. The company instituted a strategy of down-sizing prior to an impending profit downturn. Short-term performance setbacks did not prevent them from investing in the future. To support the strategy, GM went into debt for the first time in years. Profit performance over the past three years proves that this strategy is a success (although recently, because of the nationwide slump in automobile sales, the company has experienced a downturn).

K Mart Goes Its Own Way

Our second example, K Mart, illustrates how good strategic thinking not only changed the entire direction and outlook for the S.S.

Kresge Company, but for all retail merchandising. In the early 1960s, Kresge management perceived that the future for variety stores was limited. Management discerned that customers wanted a no-frills, mass-merchandising approach, emphasizing low prices (particularly on national brands) in freestanding department stores located in the suburbs, and with plenty of parking. This was entirely different from its own outlets—small, antiquated stores, poorly stocked, overstaffed, and located in central cities.

K Mart today is the second largest retailer in the U.S. and is considered to be the pacesetter in merchandising—even the giant Sears has emulated some of K Mart's tactics. The success of this strategy is even more apparent when one considers that W.T. Grant, S.S. Kresge (now K Mart), and F.W. Woolworth were companies of similar size with identical marketing approaches in the early 1960s. Since 1962, when its profits were less than $10 million, K Mart has seen its profits grow at nearly 30 percent a year. During this time, Woolworth has maintained its position and Grant has disappeared.

GM and K Mart have followed strategic thinking that resulted in sound bottom-line performance. It truly can be said that those industry leaders are innovators and have heeded Bernard Baruch's advice: "Never follow the crowd."

The Benefits of Planning

Managers should recognize that planning is deciding in the present what to do in the future. Dale H. Marco of Peat, Marwick, Mitchell & Co. has said, "Maybe 95 percent of all companies really don't pay much attention to the future. They react to history that is anywhere from one day to a few centuries old." Planning comprises the determination of a desired future and the steps necessary to bring it about. It is the process whereby companies reconcile their resources with their objectives and opportunities. Firms that do little forward planning tend not to take advantage of opportunities in line with the firm's resources. As a result, these enterprises are the most susceptible to being affected by the dynamic forces in their environments.

Old-style pragmatic businessmen are often suspicious about planning. Some executives maintain that "seat of the pants management and pure luck" play an important role in any business venture. We agree that luck always helps a business venture's success. However, it is our contention that the "luckiest" and most successful are those who plan carefully.

We hope we have demonstrated planning's impact on bottom-line performance. There are other, less tangible benefits that arise from good planning. Included among them are:[3]

Planning encourages systematic thinking ahead by management.

It leads to a better coordination of company efforts.

It leads to the development of performance standards control.

It causes the company to sharpen its guiding objectives and policies.

It results in better preparedness for sudden new developments.

It brings about a more vivid sense in the participating executives of their interacting responsibilities.

Any corporation can take the first step toward creating the missing link: a soundly conceived and implemented approach to balancing short-term results with long-range plans through meaningful measurement and evaluation of the plan itself. Without such an approach, corporate long-range performance is doomed to isolation and limited success.

[3] Melville C. Branch, *The Corporate Planning Process* (New York: American Management Association, 1962), pp. 48–49.

A CLEAR UNDERSTANDING OF
YOUR OWN INVOLVEMENT

It is not enough to be busy—the question is, what are we busy about?
                                                            —H. D. THOREAU

One of the principal results of good planning is the ability to allocate your resources where they can have the greatest impact. Managers must establish a sense of direction in their organizations and provide a rationale to which decisions can be related and against which progress can be measured. Strategic planning is thus a mechanism for exercising leadership.

The first key element for successful planning is that you, as a manager, must believe that planning is a major management function. Without such a commitment, planning will be a meaningless exercise. Not only must every manager plan, but if planning is to be done effectively, the chief executive officer must begin the process, which then proceeds down through the levels of the management structure. As Senator Charles Percy said when he was Chairman of Bell & Howell, "My job is to build the future." This is no less true for big companies than for small ones. Contrary to popular practice, a plan should be more than the sum of its parts: at each level of management contribution, there must be value added. To do less is just an arithmetic exercise.

However, the scope and involvement in planning changes as one moves through the organizational structure. We believe that the CEO should allocate a minimum of two thirds of his time to strategic thinking, with the remaining one third spent on day-to-day operations. Division and group managers should allocate nearly half their time to strategic issues. As one moves down the organizational hierarchy, the time allocated by managers to planning diminishes according to their day-to-day involvement (see Figure 1).

Figure I. Planning involvement: ideal allocation of time (shaded area indicates time spent on planning).

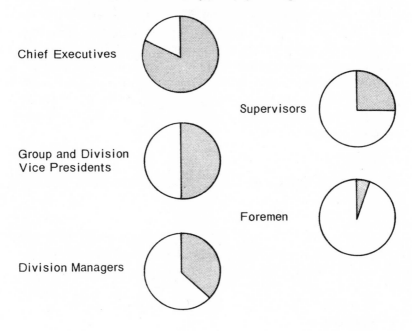

To ensure objective and fresh approaches to business opportunities and problems, it is important to separate the planning function from other corporate functions. Each business unit that is large enough to afford it should have a planner (reporting directly to the division manager) who can contact the corporate planning staff for any special projects or data needed. In smaller units, the manager may have to settle for a part-time employee for planning assistance, or he may decide that he will use all his staff to help him with his planning responsibilities.

The corporate planning staff ideally should be composed of individuals whose areas of expertise encompass economics, finance, marketing and market research, statistics and modeling, and—most important—a strategy group. The planning staff thus acts as internal consultants. We recognize that such a process will not be easy to implement, nor will it be inexpensive. For smaller companies, we recommend the use of outside services. As a final note, we suggest that periodic audits be performed by outside consultants to rejuvenate the thought process. NASA, Baxter/Travenol Laboratories, and General Electric have all used this technique with great success.

HAVING REALISTIC EXPECATIONS

Know thyself.   —SOCRATES

When embarking on a planning effort, try to avoid entrapping yourself in the three main pitfalls of planning:

The "crystal ball" syndrome
The "cure-all" syndrome
The "Persian messenger" syndrome

Some managers see planning as an effort to predict the future with some certainty as if they had a crystal ball. Unfortunately, the future is unknowable. These managers fail to comprehend that planning is a complex and integrated process of isolating and identifying individual developments that may shape the future. Out of this process, flexible action programs must be initiated to exploit the opportunities that have been uncovered. Adjustments must be made as actual events unfold, and plans must be continually monitored and updated.

Other companies are afflicted with the "cure-all" syndrome.

Overreacting, they perceive planning as a surefire answer to everyday problems. To ensure success, they place their most valued operating people in charge of the plan. Unfortunately, superior operating talent does not ensure successful planning. And good operating executives, although they clearly should be involved in planning, are still needed for operations.

Finally, one of the most difficult problems to handle is the tendency to behead the bearer of bad tidings (the "Persian messenger" syndrome). It was a pastime popular with the kings of old. But modern managers need to know what is happening, even if the news is bad. According to William S. Woodside, President of American Can, "You should lean over backwards to reward the guy who is first with the bad news." The purpose of planning is to identify both opportunities and problems within a time frame that allows development and implementation of action programs.

Planning cannot solve your problems. But it can help you focus on what the problems and opportunities are, to consider the reasonable responses, and to make better decisions about the future of your organization than would otherwise be possible.

SETTING TIME HORIZONS

Do what you can with what you have, where you are.
—T. ROOSEVELT

Let us begin by cautioning against embarking on a crash program. Initially, it is important to decide on the most appropriate time horizon for your business. For instance, natural resource companies (paper, mining, and energy) need a time horizon that often spans as much as 25 to 50 years. Other industries, such as toys, foods, snowblowers and garden implements, and clothiers, need to plan on a much shorter horizon—perhaps only one year or one season ahead.

A survey of 420 companies by the National Planning Commission showed the following distribution of planning periods:

	Percentage of companies
5 years only	53
10 years only	11
More than 10 years	6

A time frame should be chosen if it makes the greatest sense in view of the company's operating cycle and environment. A company should plan for periods greater than what appears economically justifiable. It seems foolhardy for management to make capital decisions solely on the basis of economic life. Consideration must be given to market position, environment, and the changing dynamics as the two interact.

A perfect example of such shortsightedness is a response we received from a senior executive in a natural resources company when we posed the question, "Why are you not investing in future mineral reserves, in view of the fact that it is likely that your current reserves will be exhausted in seven to ten years, and your competitors have actively been buying options to purchase all remaining reserves in your mining area?" His reply was, "Reserve investments do not demonstrate good discounted cash flows." Given the time horizon, a poor discounted cash flow seemed normal to us, so we asked, "Have you thought about what the present value is of being out of business in less than 10 years?"

Not only must you carefully choose a planning time horizon, you must also consider the time necessary for implementation of a planning process. From our experience, it takes at least two or three years to install an effective planning system that is useful to all levels and activities within the company. This time period is actually composed of two parts: development and manning, and implementation.

It has been our experience that a good planning cycle should be composed of two elements—a short-range view (up to five years), from which operating plans are set; and a long-range strategic horizon. The short-range plan centers on your immediate business cycle and is based on the assumptions used in identifying your long-range opportunities.

Most planning people will tell you that this should be an annual process. We disagree: the short-range plan should be flexible enough to adapt to short-run perturbations in the operating environment while remaining focused on the long-range objectives. Periodic review of the company's long-range plan is important, but it need not be done on a fixed calendar basis. The trigger mechanism for review of the long-range plan centers on changes in corporate goals, emerging technological innovation, changes in the market environment (governmental or competitive), and changes in consumer demographics and outlook. Once a change has been instituted in the long-range plan, you must make an immediate reassessment of the short-term plan. Let us emphasize that the short-term plan should follow your business. (This may result in more than one planning cycle per fiscal year.) Regardless of how many times a short-term plan is generated, it should always be done within the context of your long-range objectives.

A SET OF DIAGNOSTIC TOOLS

To be conscious that you are ignorant is a great step to knowledge. —BENJAMIN DISRAELI

Summarizing the major points we have addressed, let us close with a simple checklist for keeping your planning on target.

• *Stay flexible.* Too many plans suffer from inflexibility once they have been generated. The world will change and be different from what you expected, no matter how carefully you have planned.

• *Maintain a balanced outlook.* Reaction time must be geared to an understanding of your business cycle and the situation. You need not overreact, but you cannot afford to be too slow in responding, either.

• *Get top management involved.* Success hinges on the support and involvement of the CEO and his people.

• *Be critical of your assumptions and forecasts.* Data lends itself to interpretation and is only as good as the mind of the interpreter.

• *Don't focus on today.* Operating managers need to get away from everyday activities so they can step back and view the big picture.

• *Remember that only operating people can plan.* Expose your operating people to the rigors of formal thinking through a joint effort with the staff planners.

Planning is not a corporate stepchild. Rather it is a vital part of the management process.

3

PLANNING — Business Style (Part 1)

The great God Ra whose shrine once covered acres,
Is filler now for crossword puzzle makers. —KEITH PRESTON

THE PIECES OF THE PUZZLE

The objective of the planning process is to allocate resources toward strategies. The thought process, which we will describe, is intended to help managers assess plans in terms of business area, strategy, financing, and risk. The process begins with management's determination of the directions it wants the company to move in. To start this decision-making process, you must first collect information about business areas and product life cycles. From this information, each business area can be assessed for competitive position, which will enable the selection of appropriate strategies. Each strategy can serve as a framework for developing specific action plans (tactics), which will lead to the specification of associated program expenditures and risks.

Planning is necessary because of the complexities of today's business environment. The economic problems facing the world appear to be nearly insurmountable. The American economy, which is an integral part of the Free World's economy, remains in the grip of ever-present inflation, while unemployment remains at levels once regarded as unacceptable. Expenditures for energy consumption weigh heavily on our minds and finances. Raw materials are in short supply, owing to the establishment of producer cartels and rising production costs.

During the postwar period, forecasting was simple—everything pointed to continued growth. However, in today's environment, uncertainty is the norm: uncertainty about the U.S. economy, uncertainty about continued energy supplies at a reasonable price, uncertainty about continued economic growth, and uncertainty about government direction. Industrial economics are at the threshold of a new era. Perhaps never before has industry faced so many problems at once, while at the same time the future holds such promise. Superior planning, research, and management will be required to solve the market problems ahead and to realize the opportunities for the future.

There are effective ways to manage change that call for new skills in planning business development in any stage. The initial steps for a multiunit corporation are identifying the business areas that comprise the multiunit corporation; and deciding what the co-mixture of these units should be.

A multibusiness company seeks to maximize performance by achieving the best fit of divergent units. Each possible permutation has its own characteristics and capabilities. While the multibusiness company seeks to maximize its leverage, balance, and diversity, the single-product company seeks to do things in the single best way. Unfortunately, too many companies still try to treat a diversified operation as though it were a single-product firm.

We intend to present a formal but simple approach to planning for successful change in a changing environment. Such an approach enables management to control change without either sacrificing heterogeneity or agreeing on some common filter for all units. In formal planning, management runs on a perpetual track, asking specific questions and getting objective answers to each. The key questions in applying this approach are the following:

What are we?
1. Defining the distinct business areas in which the company is involved
2. Identifying the positions of these distinct business areas in terms of their product life cycles
3. Characterizing their competitive positions

What's our environment? What do we want to be?
4. Estimating potential: what can be accomplished with the resources the firm can muster within the limits imposed by our environment
5. Developing strategic goals and objectives
6. Analyzing financial and managerial liquidity

How do we get there? How do we know when we've arrived?
7. Determining strategic risk
8. Designing a managerial structure
9. Allocating resources
10. Measuring progress

Further questions to ask
What are our strengths and weaknesses?
What can we expect from what we are currently doing?
How should we change what we are doing in order to do some things better?
How are we performing?
What do we harvest and what do we grow?

This is a dynamic and never-ending process. The appropriate and correct plan for yesterday will occasionally be rendered useless by a newly discovered internal factor (a strength or weakness, possibly a technological breakthrough in a key product area) or by a change in the external environment (such as a competitive move into a key market). A good manager not only plans, but he constantly reassesses those plans while remaining alert to opportunities. These opportunities are then evaluated against his objective assessment of the company's strengths and weaknesses, resulting in a rational decision on whether or not to pursue the opportunity in the appropriate time frame. This process can be initiated only after a manager has asked himself the simple question, "What are we?"

DEFINING YOUR COMPANY

When you have eliminated the impossible, whatever remains, however improbable, must be the truth.

—SHERLOCK HOLMES
(*Sir Arthur Conan Doyle*)

Distinct Business Areas

The most difficult step in strategic planning often is defining exactly what businesses your company has. In a single-product company, this step may be relatively simple, but most companies are multiunit and for them the process is more difficult. The first and most critical step in the process is identifying distinct business areas. General Electric recognized this difficulty in the late 1960s. At that time, the company organized its businesses into more than 40 strategic areas. Today, 49 strategic business units have been grouped in sectors based on technological and market similarities.

In a multiunit corporation, a distinct business area comprises independent products or product lines that are classified according to market target, price, quality, and competition from other units in the firm. It is from these business areas that information is collected and from which strategic goals and objectives are formed. It is more difficult to define such business units than it first appears to be. In many corporations, distinct business areas are found to exist at different organizational levels. The accepted principles of categorizing organizational units into cost, profit, and divisional centers further hinders such identification. However, it is imperative that distinct business areas be identified to achieve maximum utilization of the market planning and investigation process. Of course, some companies with a narrow product range or limited markets consist of a single distinct business area. If your company fits this description, proceed as if you were a manager of a business unit in a more diverse company.

Many operating managers find themselves managing two or more business areas. The different requirements of each business area may impede market planning, development, and actions. In the plant nutrient business, for example, companies have tended to view nutrients in terms of the farmer. Yet many nutrient product lines have been extended into the consumer/homeowner area. For management to accept the notion that these new products make up a distinct business area is difficult when the consumer business end of the market is still a relatively small portion of the total business.

However, further development of these consumer markets calls for different skills than are currently available. At present, nutrient companies are geared to large volume sales of relatively undifferentiated products to a relatively knowledgeable customer. The consumer market requires a different approach: not only must brand identification be established, but along with such a program, the market manager must educate the potential customer.

We would like to be able to present a formalized approach to this, but each application must be tailor-made. For example, distinct business areas might hinge on technology or on customer grouping (consumer vs. industrial) or on resource dependence. Each business unit should have the potential to be a stand-alone business. GE defines a strategic business unit (SBU) as "a unit whose manager has complete responsibility for integrating all functions into a strategy against an identifiable external competitor."

Product Life Cycle

After the natural business areas have been classified, the next step is to determine where the product lines of each busines area fit in a normal competitive life cycle. In general terms, business areas should be segregated into the classical four stages of development: the initial, growth, mature, and decaying stages (see Figure 2). A business in the initial stage (for example, electronic measuring devices) can be characterized by fluidity, rapid growth, and volatile market shares. This type of business needs flexible and risk-taking management. A growth business such as minicomputers is one in which market size is growing, but markets, shares, and technology are defined, and barriers to entry are beginning to be established. A mature business, such as steel, is generally characterized by stability in size, market share, and technology. A decaying business (for example, automobile convertible tops) is best characterized by narrow profit margins, falling demand, and declining competition.

For instance, the medical supply industry exhibits all the characteristics of a growth industry as compared with those of a mature industry such as plant nutrients. Strategic and market planning in this environment must be longer range. Management style is more leadership-dependent and flexible than in the plant nutrient business, which tends to be bureaucratized and controlled. Growth for medical products and services is greater than the GNP growth rate, whereas growth for plant nutrients approximates the GNP rate.

In a growth company, there are fewer policies and procedures

Figure 2. Life cycle of a business.

Category	Characteristics			
Market	High Growth/ Low Share	High Growth/ High Share	Low Growth/ High Share	Low Growth/ Low Share
Financial	Cash hungry Low reported earnings Good P/E High debt level	Self-financing, cash hungry Good to low reported earnings High P/E Low-moderate debt level	Cash rich High earnings Fair P/E No debt-High debt	Fair cash flow Low earnings Low P/E Low debt capacity
Title	Embryonic	Growth	Mature	Aging
Volume growth rate	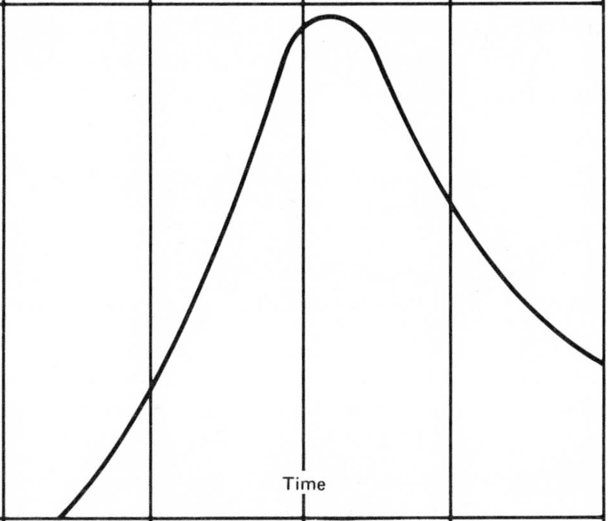			
Managerial style	Entrepreneur	Sophisticated manager	Critical administrator	Opportunistic

than in a mature business area. Communications are more informal and less uniform. Control is less fixed and more flexible. In essence, because of the growth position of the marketplace and the product life cycle, there is more freedom of movement and action in the medical industry than in a mature business, such as the plant nutrient industry. Table 2 will help identify characteristics and appropriate strategies within the life cycle stages.

Remember that careful analysis of your company and its competitive position is necessary to make an appropriate choice of strategies. For example, consider the Bowmar Instrument Company, which was one of the first participants in the calculator business (Texas Instruments was a late entry). Unfortunately for Bowmar, it lacked the necessary financial resources to fund both marketing programs and the research necessary to stay in the forefront of technological change. Also, Bowmar was financially unable to integrate vertically, so it had to purchase its microprocessor chips from outside vendors (Texas Instruments was one). Thus, TI

Table 2. Characteristics of various life cycle stages and strategies appropriate to them.

Life Cycle Stage	Characteristics	Strategies
Initial	Little or no competition High prices Limited distribution	Create consumer awareness Concentrate on quality and reliability Secure distribution
Growth	More competitors Falling prices Rapid advances in product technology	Efficient manufacturing to reduce costs Create brand loyalty Technological innovation
Maturity	Sales and volume growth slows Competitor shakeout Pricing based on cost	Increased promotion Increased financial controls Controlled inventory
Decay	Narrow product line Selective market participation Capital investment centers on maintenance	Reduced promotion Minimal capital investment Harvest cash

had both a cost advantage and a technological advantage in addition to its financial and distribution strengths. Today, Bowmar has filed for bankruptcy and is out of the calculator business, while TI dominates that industry.

Competitive Position

Once distinct business areas have been classified into developmental stages, the next critical step is the appraisal of competitive position. It is useful to think of the competitive position of a distinct business area as being one of the following: dominant, strong, advantageous, vulnerable, or insignificant. Knowing where one stands with respect to the competition is essential for determining the strategic options available. A business in a dominant market position can influence the behavior of its competition and has a wide range of options open to it. A business with a strong position can maintain an independent stance or take action without facing significant loss of market share. The factors that have to be evaluated in determining market strength include:

Market share and position
Pricing policy
Type and degree of integration
Financial position
Product mix
Technological capability
Marketing capabilities

A manager should assess his distinct business area by asking questions divided up into three general areas:

Industry profile
Business area market profile
Competitive position grid

A formal series of outward-looking general questions helps determine overview of an industry, or an "industry profile." Questions such as those shown on the "Industry Profile" below should be completed by managers within each distinct business area.

Once you have the industry in perspective, the next step is to form a general profile of the distinct business area. This is necessary to assess your competitive position in the marketplace.

INDUSTRY PROFILE

Distinct business area designation _____

Industry served _____

1. Define the market that you serve.
2. Approximately how many competing businesses are there in your served market?
3. What are the names and market shares (volume and dollar basis) of your major competitors for the last five business cycles?
4. Are there any constraints on your major competitors, such as legal, marketing, or supply?
5. During the past three to five years, has the total number of competitors been increasing or decreasing? (Identify those that have either entered or exited.) Which companies appear likely to enter the market? Which companies (or kinds of companies) are capable of entering this market?
6. Have there been any events that have significantly changed the market structure?
7. Who are the price leaders, if any? (Identify the firms that lead the way in price increases or decreases. The majority of the remaining firms usually follow at least the direction of the price leader's price changes.)
8. What is the degree of integration—forward, backward, and horizontal—for major competitors? (For example, are the leaders integrated from raw material to final product)?
9. What are the critical ingredients for success in this industry—price, service, technology, marketing, production efficiency, quality, or advertising?
10. What are the key factors influencing the growth of the industry?

11. What are the barriers to entry, such as sophisticated technology, high initial investment, or need for raw material supply?
12. Is technology an important factor? Why?
13. What is the industry's vulnerability to substitute products?
14. What is the industry's vulnerability to new products?
15. What is the industry's average percentage of production capacity utilization?
16. What is the optimum percentage of production capacity utilization for an average-size plant?
17. What is the minimum amount of additional production capacity that it is practical to add, and what is the smallest-size new plant that is economically feasible to operate?
18. What is the time required to build and bring additional production capacity on line and to start up a new plant?
19. What competitors are planning new production capacity, when, and how much?
20. What are the main product distribution channels from manufacturer to customer?
21. Are there any operating community or regulatory constraints?
22. Are there any raw materials constraints? Where do you get them? How secure is the supply?
23. What are the expense-to-sales ratios for advertising and R&D? What are gross margins, pre-tax margins, and after-tax margin? (If possible, include the latest industry ratios generated by outside sources such as Dun & Bradstreet and *Dun's Review*.)
24. Is the labor force considered to be highly technical? Is this a labor-intensive industry?
25. Are unions a major factor in the labor force?
26. What is the breakdown between domestic and overseas business?

DISTINCT BUSINESS AREA PROFILE

Distinct business area designation _____

Industry served _____

1. Describe concisely the total market and that segment in which the business area operates.
2. What is the size of the total market and the size of the segment in which you compete (if different) in units and dollars for the last five years?

3. What is the real rate of market growth over the past five years in units and dollars (by segment, if necessary)? Estimate replacement market vs. real growth.
4. What is your estimate of the future growth potential of this marketplace? On what assumptions do you base this estimate?
5. What are the categories of customers served: consumers, retailers, wholesalers, further converters of product?
6. Identify customers by category and industry.
7. Define the concentration of customer base along such lines as demographic, geographic, or business characteristics (for example, 80 percent of the customers are in the northeastern United States, or have sales in the $1–10 million range).
8. Define the degree of customer concentration (usually about 20 percent of the customer's account for 80 percent of sales). Who are the key customers?
9. What leading economic indicators are particularly important to forecasting future performance in this industry—housing starts, interest rates, disposable personal income?
10. Define the served market for this business area. Delineate by geography, channels of distribution, type of retail outlet, type of product.
11. What was your market share (volume and dollar basis) for the last five calendar years? Has it been growing, declining, or remaining stable?
12. What do you estimate your market share to be for each of the next five years?
13. Estimate the percentage of total business area sales accounted for by products introduced during the past three years.
14. What is the breadth of your product line compared with that of your competitors—less broad, of the same breadth, or broader?
15. What is the total number of products you offer? How many products generate 50 percent of your business?
16. Identify your products in terms of their life cycle position.
17. Categorize your products into branded or commodity segments (all competing brands have essentially the same performance characteristics) of specialty (indicate unique values offered).
18. Estimate the percentage of your sales volume accounted for by products and services that, from the customer's perspective, are assessed as "superior," "equivalent," and "inferior" to those available from your leading competitors.
19. What are the business area's strengths and weaknesses (technology, marketing, patents, field service, distribution)?
20. To what extent does the market value your corporate or brand

name relative to those of your major competitors (above, equal to, or below major competitors)?

21. What are your business area's main product distribution channels to your consumer?
22. What is the business area's degree of integration—forward, backward, and horizontal?
23. What is the business area's current percentage of production capacity utilization?
24. What is the business area's optimum percentage of production capacity utilization?
25. Are there other profitable alternative uses of excess production capacity?
26. What is the business area's operating cost position compared with that of your competitors?
27. How does your financial performance compare with, your major competitors (higher, equivalent, or lower) in pre-tax return on average assets, interest as a percentage of average assets, and average asset turnover?
28. How does your market performance compare with that of your major competitors (higher, equivalent, or lower) in gross margin, pre-tax return on sales, advertising as a percentage of sales, R&D as a percentage of sales, and sales expense as a percentage of sales?

Not only must you concentrate on your present competitors; you must also look at the total competition. Don't forget to include potential entrants into the market. Remember, competition can arise through numerous forms—direct or indirect. For example, a direct competitor of A&P is Safeway; however, an indirect competitor is the entire restaurant industry. The same situation arises in individual products. A good illustration can be found in the shoe industry. For years, leather manufacturers had a monopoly on the raw material inputs in shoe manufacturing. They considered their prime competition to be other domestic leather tanneries. With the advent of synthetic materials and foreign tanning operations, the market structure changed dramatically. Because they were not prepared for this change in competition, U.S. tanning operations today are barely viable.

After answering the complete list of questions which explores the future environment, compile a grid that summarizes all the data collected. We suggest the format shown on the following pages (Competitive Position Analysis Worksheet). You may adapt it to fit your particular needs.

COMPETITIVE SUMMARY

"Do you personally have difficulty making decisions?" "Well, yes and no!"
                                                    —ANONYMOUS

After completing the competitive position analysis and grid, you should be able to determine your distinct business area's competitive position. On the basis of your assessments and interpretation, rank your company or your area using the scheme shown in Table 3. (We realize that decisions are always made on incomplete data and subjective assessment is necessary. Nevertheless, a choice must be made.)

During each business cycle, the operating business area manager should position his business area into the competitive grid shown in Table 4. The indicators given in the table are only a sample of the factors we have presented. Business area A appears to be in a weak competitive position, while business area B appears to have a strong position. The business area doing the analysis is clearly in a shaky position. A possible reason indicated by this analysis is an excessively broad range of products. But of course this is only a clue for further analysis.

Another useful tool is matrix analysis. In this analysis, the position of each distinct business area is placed on a matrix according to its relative share of the market and the relative rate of growth of the market it is in. The ideal position, of course, is for your business area to have high market share in a market with a high rate of

Table 4. Analysis of competitor market strengths.

Competitive Indicators	Major Competitors				Business Area
	A	B	C	D	
Market position	Vulnerable	Dominant	Strong	Vulnerable	Vulnerable
General trend (in market position)	Steady	Steady	Up	Down	Down
Profitability (low, average, high)	Low	Average	Average	Average	Low
Financial strength (low, average, high)	Low	High	Unknown	Low	Low
Product mix (broad, narrow)	Narrow	Broad	Narrow	Narrow	Extensive
Technological capability (strong, weak, average)	Average	Strong	Average	Weak	Average
Cost outlook (favorable, unfavorable)	Unfavorable	Favorable	Favorable	Unfavorable	Unfavorable
Quality (good, satisfactory, minimum)	Minimum	Good	Satisfactory	Minimum	Satisfactory
Product development (good, satisfactory, minimum)	Minimum	Good	Satisfactory	Satisfactory	Good

you either in analyzing your business portfolio or in comparing your own business to other businesses within your company or industry.

WHAT'S YOUR ENVIRONMENT?

Once you have assessed your resources and determined where you are (competitive position, technology, human and other resources),

Competitive Position Analysis Worksheet

Description	Your Business Area	Major Competitors (Name)	Potential Competitors
Percentage of market share (most recent business cycle) Volume basis Dollar basis			
Change in market share (past 5 years; increasing or decreasing)			
Estimated market share (next 3 business cycles) Volume basis Dollar basis			
Indicate price leader, if any			
Indicate high, average, or low: Forward integration Backward integration			
Indicate current percentage of production capacity utilization			
Rate the financial characteristics that relate to competitive success: Profitability (high, average, or low) Cash availability (high, average, or low) Other: Other:			

Estimate percentage of sales accounted for by new products introduced in last three years

Product mix (broad or narrow)

Estimate percentage of sales accounted for by products assessed by customers as:
Superior
Equivalent
Inferior

Degree of customer concentration (many or few)

Strength of corporate/brand name (strong or weak)

Operating cost position (favorable or unfavorable)

Financial performance vs. major competitors (higher, equivalent, or lower)
Pre-tax return on invested capital
Interest as percentage of invested turnover (include coverage ratio)
Average assets turnover
Inventory turnover
Leverage ratios (debt/equity)
Depreciation vs. capital expenditures
Cash flow

Market performance vs. major competitors (higher, equivalent, or lower)
Advertising expenditures as percentage of sales

R&D expenditures as percentage of sales
Pre-tax earnings as percentage of sales
Gross margins

Description	Your Business Area	Major Competitors (Name)	Potential Competitors
Technological innovation and capability (strong, weak, or average)			
Product development (good, satisfactory, minimum)			
Percentage of business generated (attach breakdown by area) Domestic Nondomestic			
List critical ingredients for success, and rate each of your competitors and your business area as dominant, strong, advantageous, vulnerable, or insignificant. These ingredients might include Quality Reputation Service Brand identification Labor relations			

Table 3. Determining the competitive position of your company or business area.

Competitive Strategic Position	Definition
1. Dominant	Controls behavior of other competitors (performance and/or strategy). Has a wide choice of strategic options (widest choice of options both natural and selected).
2. Strong	Able to take independent stance or action without endangering long-term position. Able to maintain long-term position regardless of competitors' actions.
3. Advantageous	Has a strength which is exploitable in particular strategies. Has a greater than average opportunity to improve position.
4. Vulnerable	Sufficiently satisfactory performance to warrant continuation in business. Usually exists at the sufferance of the dominant company or the industry in general. Has a less than average opportunity to improve position.
5. Insignificant	Currently unsatisfactory performance, but opportunity exists for improvement. May have most of characteristics of better position, but obvious shortcomings. Inherently short-term condition; usually must change—either grow or disappear.

growth. This is the kind of business that offers the greatest opportunities, and is clearly a "star." The simplest matrix is the one developed by the Boston Consulting Group, shown in Figure 3.

Matrix analysis is most useful in comparing your distinct business areas to determine if you have a good balance of businesses. You usually need cash cows to finance the wildcat businesses in order to make them into stars and to develop your stars. Usually you will want to get rid of your "dogs." Sometimes they can be turned into stars by foreseeable market changes or technological

Figure 3. A simple matrix analysis.

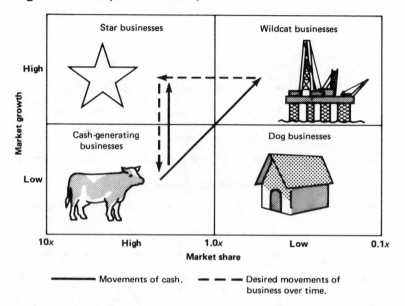

Movements of cash.   — — — Desired movements of business over time.

breakthroughs. A matrix analysis is, therefore, just a tool helpful to the next step is to forecast the environment you will be operating in. The environment restricts your choices as to what you can do in the future. It also gives you your opportunities for expansion and new directions. For this reason, accurate forecasts are essential.

Unfortunately, the future is unknowable. We therefore have to make what we believe to be reasonable assessments on the basis of reasonable assumptions about the future. The longer the period of the forecast, the more difficult it is to be confident about our projections. We feel more secure about our estimates of production requirements for next week than we do about our total market for next year. Similarly, we are more comfortable with that estimate of next year's market than we are about forecasts of how changes in the market will affect acceptability of our product five years from now.

The time span required for environmental forecasts varies depending on your industry. If you are in the women's fashion industry, your effective forecasting requirement may be two seasons ahead—less than a year. A food processor may be able to develop, test, and establish a market in a new product within five years; thereby making that the required forecasting time. A chemical company's forecast may have to be 15 years ahead to cover development and testing of a product, pilot production, and building a plant. Mining companies must forecast over 20–25 year spans, and lumber products companies must encompass 40–50 years, the time it takes to grow a harvestable tree. Your forecasts should cover:

1. The overall economy
2. Your industry
   Customers: their number and needs; likely new customers; likely new uses of your products; customers who will cease to be customers, and for what reasons.
   Competitors: existing ones; those who are exiting; those likely to enter the market in the future; competitors that will be created because their new products will substitute for your present products.
3. Social and political trends
4. Demographics of your market
5. Government regulations: environmental, safety, tax laws, and so on
6. Material supply
7. Distribution

8. Labor requirements and availability
9. Financial requirements and availability of funds
10. Technology: trends, likely changes, impact on your markets

Of course, the specific information you will need for your forecast will vary with your industry. In a high-technology market such as minicomputers, the technology forecast may be the key to your success. If a new form of memory is introduced by your competitors before you can equal or improve on it, you may be out of business. In an industry such as soft drinks, the demographics of the population are key. Soft drinks are consumed primarily by teenagers. The distribution of our population is such that the number of teenagers will be dropping rapidly over the next decade. Soft drink manufacturers must therefore find new markets, take market share from competitors, accept a contraction of business, or go into different markets. For example, Coca-Cola, seeing this change in demographics, has gone into the wine business by purchasing Taylor Wines. Wine is consumed mainly by young adults. Coca-Cola hopes to hold on to its present customers when they leave their teens by selling a product that will replace soft drinks as their beverage of choice.

To make reasonable forecasts, you must have a great deal of information about your market, your industry, and the world outside your industry. You must read extensively, attend meetings both in your industry and in a broader area, and talk with people who have a broad range of knowledge and interests. This is not as difficult as it may first appear to be. If you have a planning department or a corporate library, you can get a great deal of assistance from them. If you don't, you will have to do your own digging. This may prove to be valuable enough to warrant the extra time expended, since you will not have somebody else filtering the information you get. A junior staff person is likely to take a shorter and narrower view of the world than you will require for your planning. (In the back of this chapter is a list of some of the more readily available sources of information and some suggestions for seeking the information that is key in your own industry.)

We recommend that you always cross-reference your information in order to determine validity and accuracy. On more than one occasion, we have found that experts have been known to err. Also, it is important never to discount your in-house expertise.

We caution against interpreting the information to fit your needs. A brief anecdote illustrates our point. A senior executive at a chemicals company had overall responsibility for distinct business areas competing in agricultural and industrial chemicals. Upon review of the competitive position analysis of one of his DBAs, a $50 million specialty chemicals company competing directly with Du Pont, he made the following statement: "We spend more after-tax earnings per dollar on R&D than does Du Pont."

We tried to convince him that in absolute dollars, a $700,000 R&D budget versus Du Pont's more than $300 million budget made for no meaningful comparison. However, he maintained that his spending of 70 percent of after-tax profits on R&D would provide him with the technological breakthroughs necessary to outflank Du Pont in the marketplace. "Perhaps you are expecting too much from your R&D effort," we cautioned. "It might be more advantageous for you to concentrate on marketing, as well as the development of 'me-too' products."

A period of two years elapsed in which we noticed almost a total reduction in basic research spending, with no corresponding shift to either a marketing emphasis or the development of "me-too" products. Today, his company finds itself with shrinking market share, no new products, a dissatisfied customer base, and no brand identification. That DBA's survival is now in doubt.

WHAT DO YOU WANT TO BE?

"Cheshire Puss," (Alice) began, ". . . would you please tell me which way I ought to go from here?" "That depends on where you want to get to," said the Cat. "I don't much care where . . .," said Alice. "Then it doesn't matter which way you go," said the Cat.

—LEWIS CARROLL
Alice in Wonderland

When you are satisfied that your assessment of the future is as good as it can be, the next step is to select the position you want for the future. This is not an easy task. Consider the General Electric Company. After carefully reviewing the company's position in the late 1960s and early 1970s, GE management determined that, despite the company's apparent success, it would be necessary to redirect its efforts to achieve real success. In the growth period of the 1960s, GE's businesses turned in record sales performances. But upon close inspection, management discovered that this growth was, in fact, "profitless."[1] Investments were yielding sales growth without commensurate earnings gains, causing return on investment to decline.

The profit disappointments from GE's investments suggested that flaws existed in the company's approach to investment decision making and resource allocation. This exprience underscored the need to be more selective in the allocation of resources. GE recognized that, for a diversified company, some operations can be best served by generating earnings, while others with strong growth prospects offer better investment opportunities over the

[1] Michael G. Allen, "Diagramming GE's Planning for What's Watt," *Planning Review*, September 1977.

long run. Given this realization and the corporate objectives of re-
taining a "one company" image in which profitability and return
on investment remain at healthy levels, GE established an organization centered on so-called "strategic business units" and emphasizing planning. Today, GE appears to be maintaining its leadership position as an integrated and innovative multinational
corporation built up from its base of electrical goods and ma-
chinery.

Unfortunately, not all companies can assess their positions un-
emotionally. For example, Abercrombie & Fitch, founded in 1892,
made its name by catering to an affluent, elitist clientele drawn by
the store's expensive, high-quality sports equipment, apparel, and
gifts. A&F outfitted Theodore Roosevelt's African safaris and Ad-
miral Richard Byrd's expedition to Antarctica. Although it eventually expanded into a chain with branches in nine cities and attempted to broaden its product line, A&F never adapted to
modern-style retailing or to a younger, more budget-conscious
generation of activists who preferred to buy from department
stores and discounters.

When additional volume failed to materialize, the company
ran into working-capital problems. Sales peaked at $28 million in
1968, then tumbled steadily to less than $20 million annually. In
1975, the company lost $1 million; in August 1976, it filed for
bankruptcy. Only during the liquidation sale did the venerable retailer attract the kinds of crowds it needed to survive: within two
weeks, 40 percent of the inventory had been sold. Abercrombie &
Fitch never addressed the critical question: can a purveyor of elitist
values also be a mass merchandiser? Perhaps rather than opening
numerous stores, A&F should have concentrated on selectivity in
location and services. For example, would it not have been a natural offshoot for A&F to organize the expeditions and vacations for
which they outfitted their customers?

We have already mentioned the railroads, which decided that what they wanted was to be railroads rather than diversified transportation companies. A history of bankruptcies suggests that this may not have been the right answer (although particularly bad management has certainly been a factor in the bankruptcies of many railroads).

In another part of the transportation industry—automobiles—GM is dominant, Ford is strong, and Chrysler and AMC are vulnerable. Chrysler and AMC have distinctly different ideas of what they want to be. Chrysler wants to be a producer of mass market automobiles in direct competition with GM and Ford. Its efforts have not been particularly successful, as it has seen its market share slowly erode over the past several years, and only through government guarantees has the company not fallen into bankruptcy.

Trying to compete with GM in every market niche proved to be a task larger than Chrysler's resources could fund. Because capital was diverted to international ventures (which were significant losers when they were acquired and which remained that way), Chrysler had few resources with which to respond to the dramatic changes in American buying habits that occurred as a result of rapidly rising fuel prices. Even Chrysler's new management refuses to see the value of selective competition, which is the only way the company will be "saved."

AMC, on the other hand, looked at the same competitive situation and decided to be a builder of specialty cars for a select small segment of the market. This was successful when AMC was the only manufacturer of small cars, until the larger companies moved into the market. Production of Jeeps has shown continuing success. The Pacer, a recent special car, has not proved particularly successful. But AMC's consistent self-image has certainly helped it to survive in its precarious market position.

SETTING OBJECTIVES AND GOALS

Having lost sight of our objective, we redoubled our efforts.

—OLD ADAGE

Setting goals is the most important task a management performs. The most effective leaders are those who work with their associates to establish mutual, meaningful goals toward which the organization moves. Objectives must be set to avoid the kind of development that occurs solely as a result of random forces. Most managers recognize the importance of objectives, which are the fundamental strategies of the business derived from what the business is and what it should be. However, few managers identify and structure their objectives, and then these same managers are generally dissatisfied with the results. Statements of objectives are often too vague to be of use in resolving difficult company problems. When citing their objectives, firms often do not know what they had in mind other than merely sounding virtuous. Typical examples are: "to be the best in the industry," "to strive for the most effective use of capital," or "to serve the common good."

Goals and Objectives

In an article published in *Planning Review* discussing the difference between goals and objectives, Malcolm W. Pennington, president of The Marketing Planning Group, Inc., stated:

> The glossary of planning is by no means widely agreed upon, but a reasonably consistent distinction is developing between the meaning of the words "objectives" and "goals." Objectives can best be described as the broad general aims of the organization, essentially a "wish list." Goals, on the other hand, are

specific targets to be reached on the way to achieving these broad objectives.[2]

As Mr. Pennington says, objectives such as to increase market share, expand into new markets, reduce costs, and increase profits are laudable, but not useful for planning because too many questions are left unanswered. To make them useful, we must state goals such as "increase in sales of 16 percent for the next five years," or "to become a major factor in the health vitamin market with a market share of at least 40 percent by 1981." For goals to be useful, they must be:

Significant
Reasonable
Challenging
Specific and measurable
Connected to a reward system
Consistent with each other

Let us now move from the abstract to the concrete. From the following actual statement of goals, can you determine what business this company is in? Where it wants to take the business? And what part the employees will play in attaining these goals?

STATEMENT OF GOALS

1. To safeguard and protect the stockholders' investments in the parent company and its subholding companies through guidance, monitoring, and controlling of operating performance of existing businesses as well as new business venture.
2. To maintain a long-term acceptable level of return on invested capital and consistent growth in earnings per share.

[2] Malcolm W. Pennington, "Go for the Goal," *Planning Review,* March 1979.

3. To increase the value of the company to its shareholders by achieving and maintaining a price/earnings ratio greater than 10:1. The company will strive to minimize the impact of major swings in earnings from volatile business segments.
4. To communicate the company's identity to the financial community.
5. To allocate capital resources to those programs that provide the means to broaden and enhance the company's capacity to participate in diverse growth businesses.
6. To pursue policies that will assure the company of the ability to raise capital on reasonable terms.
7. To provide an environment in which further capable professional management can be developed. Responsibility and accountability for achieving this goal rests jointly with subholding company and parent company management.
8. To be a progressive and responsible member of the national and world community.

In fact this company (formerly among the Dow Jones 30 Industrials) participates in food products, chemicals, oil and gas, consumer electronics, and women's personal products. But it is impossible to determine that from its statement of goals.

The following is an example of a company that has specified its objectives in detail:

STATEMENT OF BASIC PURPOSES OF THE LOCKHEED AIRCRAFT CORPORATION[3]

The basic purposes of Lockheed are:
- To be the major company satisfying in the highest technical sense the national security needs of the United States and its allies in space, air, land, and sea
- To employ technical resources in meeting the nondefense needs of governments and the requirements of commercial markets
- To achieve continuous growth of profits at a rate needed to attract and retain stockholder investment

[3] George A. Steiner, *Top Management Planning* (New York: Macmillan, 1969).

- To recognize and appropriately discharge our responsibilities for the welfare of our employees, the communities in which we do business, and society as a whole
- To maintain a large proportion of sales in advanced technical products bearing the Lockheed name
- To maintain continuity of the enterprise by holding relatively low rates of change in ownership, management, and employees

We recognize that all corporations need broad and all-encompassing objectives in their basic charters. However, the distinct business areas need to establish *specific* and *measurable* goals within the framework of the broad objectives. For goals to be successful at the DBA level, they need to be operational (capable of being converted into specific targets). Additionally, they must make it possible to concentrate resources and efforts. Selectivity is necessary. Goals must be multiple in scope and they must be interactive, allowing for strategic trade-offs. Finally, goals must concentrate upon issues necessary for the survival of the business. In general, useful goals address:

Profit requirements
Market environment
Products and product leadership
Resources—technological, physical, financial, and human
Productivity
Innovation
Social responsibility
Organizational structure

Obviously, the information generated during your analysis phase will assist in setting goals. Let us stress that goals must be measurable, time-related, reasonable, dynamic, and challenging. Goals must not only be useful for planning; more importantly, they must be useful for operating and performing. Malcolm Pennington poses the following questions to enable specific goal setting:

What is your target market share, and by what time should you reach it?

What are the new markets?

What will be your percentage of market share for these new markets—and again, by what time?

What is the specific goal for cost reduction in dollars or percentages, and when should you achieve it?

What is the figure for those increased profits, and when should you reach it?

These are tough questions, but are necessary for positioning yourself in the future. As was mentioned earlier (prior to the section on individual DBA objective setting), it is important that the CEO and the top management team, in conjunction with the board of directors, initiate overall corporate challenges. Remember: goals should not be cast in concrete nor should they be illusory. Given the challenges, the DBAs will generate their forecasts. If some divergence in expectations occurs, either corporate strategy or individual DBA strategy, or both, have to be adjusted.

HOW DO YOU GET THERE?

The determination of the basic long-range goals and objectives of an enterprise leads to the adoption of courses of action and the allocation of resources necessary for reaching these goals. A business strategy is a statement that provides a framework for formulating and classifying related action plans to achieve the business area's objective. These action plans normally call for and are supported by resource allocations. These allocations can include program expenditures for fixed assets, working capital, and operating expense items (such as new facilities, inventory expansions, and advertising expenses).

It is important to distinguish strategies, which are related to the long-term development of the business, from action plans designed to carry out the strategies. For instance, the implementation of the strategy of entering new markets might require an action plan of building a new plant in a new sales territory. In this context of business planning, traditional marketing "strategies" (such as changing the mix of advertising versus product development expenditures) are action plans and *not* business strategies. Strategy elements are functional or subfunctional actions (such as pricing, funding, make vs. buy, innovate vs. emulate) that are combined to create a business strategy. Strategy alternates are different sets of strategy elements which are combined to achieve the same essential objectives.

Robert Weinberg has identified eight basic strategic trade-offs facing any firm:[4]

1. Short-term profits vs. long-term growth
2. Profit margin vs. competitive position
3. Direct sales effort vs. market development effort
4. Penetration of existing markets vs. development of new markets
5. Related vs. nonrelated new opportunities as a source of long-term growth
6. Profit vs. nonprofit goals (that is, social responsibilities)
7. Growth vs. stability
8. "Riskless" environment vs. high-risk environment

[4] Presented in a seminar, "Developing Management Strategies for Short-Term Profits and Long-Term Growth," held at Regency Hotel, New York City, September 29, 1969. Sponsored by Advanced Management Research, Inc.

Daniel T. Carroll, former president of Gould, Inc., had clearly thought out his company's strategies, as is indicated by this passage from one of his reports to Gould's annual financial analysts' conference in New York:

> What kind of a business are we and what do we want it to do? We settled on these four elements. First, we said that Gould will use existing technological leadership and apply it to new products.
>
> Now that simple statement implies several things: We have technological skills in certain discrete areas. We intend to pursue those. They are electromechanics, electrochemistry, metallurgy, and electronics.
>
> We haven't strayed from that. As a matter of fact, when we acquired companies that possessed elements or subcomponents that were outside our element field, we have worked to dispose of them, and have made during the three years I've been with Gould, six or eight divestitures of this type. . . .
>
> Second, we seek to establish a leadership position in related markets. We realize this is not a unique concept. General Electric and many other corporations long have recognized that if you cannot obtain a leadership position you must suffer somebody else's whims for a long time to be able to achieve the kind of prices, volume, and cost-related opportunities. This desire, to establish leadership positions in related markets, brings us to the third point in the Gould concept—market-engineered products.
>
> We have tried to get out of our products market leadership through engineering content. However, if they lacked substantial engineering content, we recognize how rapidly such products can degenerate to commodity levels . . .
>
> And that brings us to the fourth portion of the Gould concept: shift product mix to emphasize higher margin lines . . .

Taken altogether, this four-part concept forms Gould's corner-stone objective—to become a product-development company.

After identifying strategies (within the framework of your position, resources, and environment), they must be evaluated. We recommend validating strategies by asking some simple questions.

1. In view of your resources, does the strategy make sense?
   (a) Do you have the necessary manpower?
   (b) Are the operating assets in place or easily accessible?
   (c) Will your capital support the strategy?
   (d) Is your timing appropriate?
2. In view of your product positioning (both life cycle and marketplace), is your strategy viable?
   (a) Have you assessed your competitive environment correctly?
   (b) Have you considered possible competitor response?
   (c) Is your distribution network realistically assessed?
3. Can the company afford the risk?
   (a) What is the impact of success or failure?
   (b) Does this strategy change the direction of your core business more than you'd like it to?
   (c) Are the predicted returns real?
   (d) Do the people responsible for implementation believe in the success of the strategy?

Is the strategy flexible enough to cope with environmental changes? Table 5 highlights the appropriate responses to particular strategies.

The following is a framework of strategic actions from which to choose. Of course, this is not an all-inclusive list, and much deliberation and thought must enter each choice. But these are the basic options that are available:

Table 5. Appropriate responses to particular strategies.

Business Area	Growth Strategy	Response to: Selective Investment Strategy	Cash Generation Strategy
Risk	Accept/contain	Limit	Avoid
Market Share	Build/diversify markets	Target growth/protect position	Forgo share for profit
Pricing	Lead; exploit cost/value elasticity	Stabilize for maximum contribution	Lag, even at the expense of volume
Products	Lead, diversify	Differentiate specialization, application, performance	Prune
Costs	Utilize scale, not thrift	Aggressive reduction of variable, economize on fixed	"Variabilize" by ruthless cutting, consolidation
Marketing	Build creativity/coverage	Cut creativity, keep coverage	Cut expenditures
Manpower	Add/develop	Limit/maintain	Attrition

Maintain business in present posture.

Prune back to a more effective business configuration. Such changes must be applied to products, markets, distribution system, R&D facilities, and all important business areas.

Survival. All decisions are determined by their immediate contribution to profit and cash flow, with little regard to any probable long-term detrimental effect.

Replacement. Improve operating efficiency through the addition or replacement of more economical equipment or facilities.

Development. Improve operating efficiency or effectiveness by the development and adoption of new ways of doing existing tasks.

Backward integration. Add functions and operations that are necessary to supply and support existing operations.

Forward integration. Add operations and functions that result in increased control over distribution and marketing functions.

Increase market share through aggressive programs such as increased advertising, lower prices, and increased service. This may lower short-term earnings.

Increase volume by entering new markets with existing products. New markets may be geographic or may be a different segment of an existing market.

Introduce new products or line extensions (developed or acquired) into existing markets.

Enter new markets (geographic or otherwise) with newly developed or acquired products.

OPERATING PLANS

A critical reason for many planning failures is the inadequate formulation of a good operating plan. In practice, a good operating plan should cover a multitude of functions. A minimum requirement for success with any operating plan is an appropriate, competent appraisal of the business potential and results of the enterprise. Organization and procedures coupled with timetables reflecting costs requirements are necessary inputs into operating plans, but you should not forget management and staff expertise. Of course, the other fundamental planning principles and guidelines that are being discussed here are additional requirements. Now let's consider a couple of examples.

Production Planning

In the late 1960s, NASA embarked on a program to design and develop a scientific instrument package to be soft-landed on Mars in time to celebrate America's 200th anniversary. A program was formulated and submitted to the aerospace industry for bidding. Subsequently Martin Marietta Corp. was awarded the contract. Even though the United States had landed an unmanned scientific program on the moon in the mid-1960s, it was recognized that the complexity of a Mars landing would tax the limit and daring of the aerospace community. A six-year, $1 billion operating plan was constructed. The plan involved thousands of people and hundreds of companies and components. The project encompassed not only industry but also research centers and major universities.

The product plan was simple in concept, but extremely complex in its application. Martin Marietta's plan incorporated all the necessary elements of any good production plan:

Design
Controls and timetables
Fabrication
All phases of assembly
Scheduling of parts and materials
Subcontracting scheduling
Quality control
Cost control
Inventory
Testing

Timetables were assigned, accompanied by cost elements. These timetables were reviewed periodically, and were tracked using management expertise, performance evaluation and review technique (PERT), and other adopted models. Figures 4 and 5 illustrate the production planning process for only two major components: the vehicle structure and the imagery (TV) experiment. Figure 6 shows some general guidelines on linking strategies with action plans.

Figure 4. Martin Marietta's production planning process for vehicle structure of the NASA Viking Lander System (VLS).

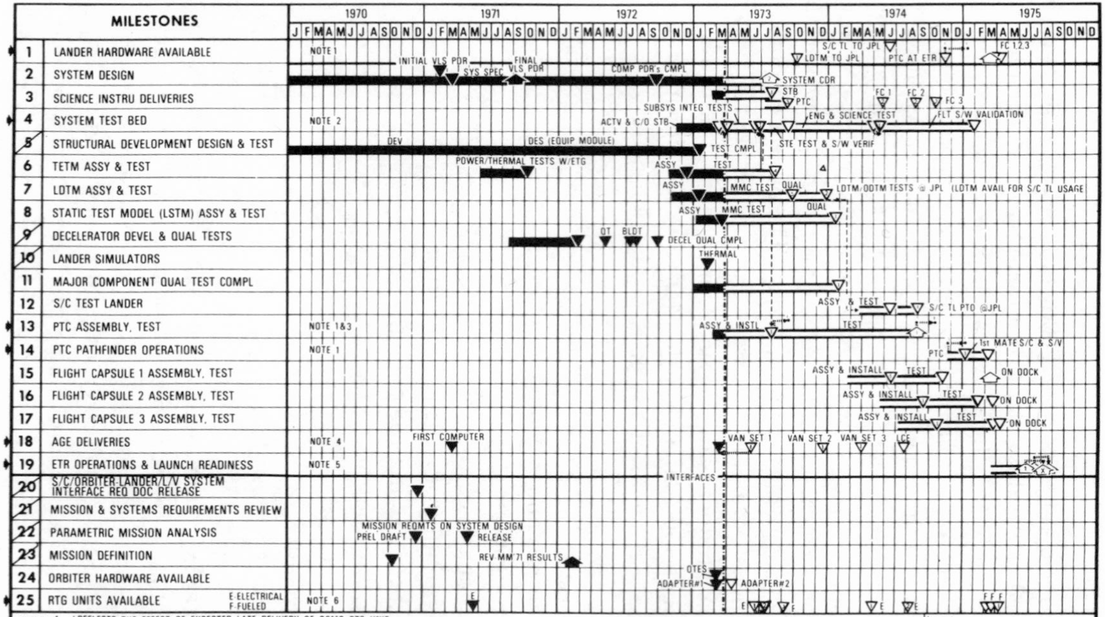

NOTES

1. REFLECTS THE EFFECT OF EXPECTED LATE DELIVERY OF GCMS PTC UNIT
2. MILESTONES RESCHEDULE RESULTING FROM STB READINESS REVIEW
3. REFLECTS THE EFFECT OF EXPECTED LATE DELIVERY OF SURFACE SAMPLER BOOM ASSY TO PTC ASSY
4. VAN #1 DELIVERED TO STB EARLIER THEN SCHEDULED TO ENABLE EARLY STB START. MODS REQUIRED FOR VAN WILL BE COMPLETED DURING STB CHECKOUT
5. LAUNCH READINESS DATES CHANGED TO REFLECT REPLAN OF ETR PRELAUNCH OPERATIONS INCORPORATING PROJECT MANAGERS RESERVE IN EARLIER ACTIVITIES
6. DELIVERY OF 2nd ETG TO MMA RESCHEDULED TO PROVIDE TIME FOR QUAL TESTING PER AEC REQUEST

Legend

E CURRENT PERT EXPECTED DATE

A SYSTEM MANAGER'S ASSESSMENT

Figure 5. Martin Marietta's production planning process for VLS imagery experiment.

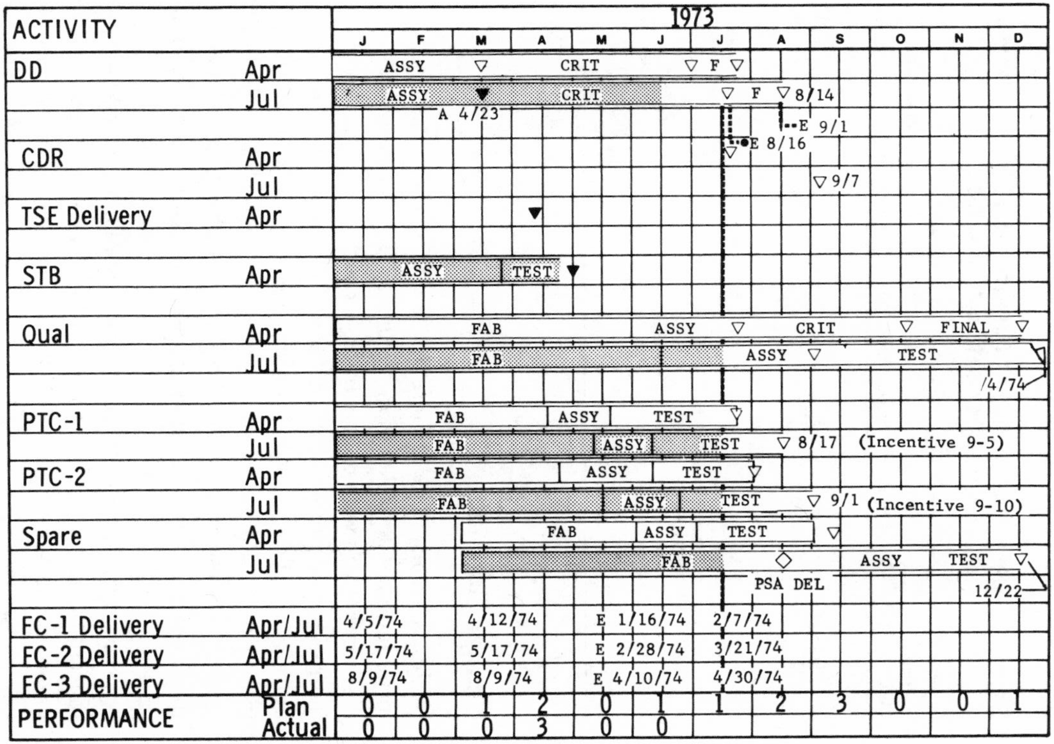

Figure 6. General guidelines to clarify the planning process of linking strategies with action plans.

Strategy (New Venture)	Course of Action	Program Expenditures	Critical Issues Environmental	Critical Issues Capital
Increase profitability of existing products by entering new markets.	1. Begin site selection in 1980.	1. New plant full production by: 1981 – $8.0 million 1982 – $2.0 million	1. Government approval.	1. After-tax rate of return – 16 percent.
	2. Start up advertising and promotion in fall of 1981.	2. 1981 – $3.0 million 1982 – $1.5 million	2. Capacity level.	2. Payback – 6 years.
			3. Account commitment and extent of orders.	3. Average return on invested capital – 20 percent.

Market Planning

In simple terms, there are just two major fundamental steps in the formulation of a market plan. First is the identification of a particular market you wish to penetrate. Second is development of a configuration and product line that must be created to compete in the market. Needless to say, in order to formulate a good marketing plan, you should have data covering the market, the competition, consumers, and management style. Only after these elements are thoroughly understood can a concise and well thought-out plan be constructed.

For example, consider the marketing plan of a well-known restaurant operation. This enterprise started as a mom-and-pop operation on the West Coast. It was noticed by a mutinational food corporation, which acquired the unit in the early 1970s. The intent was to repackage the menu and sell the new products through frozen food sections of grocery stores.

However, after acquiring the unit and performing extensive market research on the product line, the corporation realized that the restaurant had great appeal to high income groups. Recognizing this potential, the company issued guidelines for expansion of the enterprise. There were some hurdles to overcome and these were recognized by the senior management team. Some of the problems were that the operation needed high volume to justify the capital investment. Also, because of the rather unique appeal to high income groups, market penetration would be limited to select areas of the country. This required selective advertising. Finally, quality control would be paramount.

With all this in mind, the company embarked on an ambitious program: first, to recruit a competent management team; second, to develop a systematic procedure to prepare the food; third, to develop real estate expertise; and fourth, to prepare a market penetration plan.

The company chose the schedules shown in Tables 6 and 7. While each restaurant was being constructed, staff recruitment was started two months early, and workers were trained one month before the restaurant's opening. A preopening advertising campaign with billboards, radio, flyers, posters, and direct mail was initiated two weeks before the grand opening. The campaign appealed to customers within a ten-mile radius of the unit. During the first two months, discounting was encouraged to attract cus-

Table 6. Phase A: concept development, restaurant marketing plan.[1]

	1969	1970
Menu development[2]		January–March
Training procedures		March–September
Recruit core management	October–June	
Site selection: office—main first units	September–November	June–December
Design of first unit		June–December

[1] Plan put into effect August 1969.
[2] Parent company had R&D facility.

Table 7. San Francisco restaurant marketing plan.

	1970	1971
Site selection [1]	June–December	
Number of units to open		2
Date of openings		
(a) Downtown		September
(b) Oakland		December
Negotiations for sites	September	
Start meeting staff requirements		
(a) Downtown		July
(b) Oakland		October
Training schedule		
(a) Downtown		August
(b) Oakland		November
Advertising campaign [2]		
(a) Downtown		August
(b) Oakland		November

[1] Based on market analysis of community demographics.
[2] A specific advertising plan was submitted for review.

tomer attention. As of today, the company has 100 units across the
United States. Tables 6 and 7 present an overview of the market
plans.

FINANCIAL PLANS

Once strategies have been identified and selected, specific directly
related program expenditures should be developed. Since the
entire planning process is an interactive communicative process
involving appropriate key production, marketing, financial, and
R&D people, it is essential for these individuals to meet periodically to evaluate the course of action. The example shown in Figure 6 should help clarify this process of linking strategies with action plans and the related program expenditures.

After all program expenditure requests—including expenditures for fixed assets, working capital, and major operating expenses—are developed, these should be classified into contraction, maintenance, replacement, and new ventures expenditures:

Contraction involves reduction of the current configuration to a more profitable form.

Maintenance expenditures should be limited to those necessary to meet proper guidelines of health, safety requirements of government agencies, and the replacement of equipment needed to continue operation.

Replacement expenditures permit improvement of an existing operation, including the replacement of an entire facility with a new, more efficient one.

New ventures expenditures are directed toward an increase of marketing and/or manufacturing capabilities and acquisition of existing businesses or assets.

After the expenditure classification has been made, pro forma income, balance sheet, and cash flow statements to fit the action plans should be compiled by business area for each program expenditure. Along with the financials, we assume that you will generate discounted cash flows, return-on-investment projections, and payback periods (both nominal and discounted) in line with your corporate guidelines. Of course, a plan cannot be completed unless numbers that demonstrate the impact are compiled. On the following pages are examples of summary financial tables suitable for a distinct business area (see "General Planning Information" and "Financial Planning Information"). They should be modified appropriately for your own needs. This same format can be utilized for the corporate consolidation.

Consider this example. A company composed of three distinct

General Planning Information

Company _____   Cash Generation _____

Business _____   Selective Investment _____

Program _____   Growth _____

Unit No. _____

	Last Year	This Year	Plan Year 1	Plan Year 2
Revenue Volumes (000 units)				
Intercompany sales				
Trade sales				
Capital Projects and Fixed Asset Reconciliation (in dollars)				
Carryover, beginning of period				
Continuance—automotive				
Continuance—governmental				
Continuance—other				
Improvement				
Expansion				
Acquisition				
Carryover, end of year				
Total capital expenditures				
Net fixed assets, beginning of period				
Disposals—net				
Depreciation expense				
Depletion expense				
Net fixed assets, end of period				
Average trade receivables				
Average inventory				
Average current assets				
Average trade payables				
New long-term debt borrowing				
Current tax expense				
Deferred tax expense				
Total				

Columns on these two forms should be extended to include the plan for at least year 4.

Financial Planning Information

Company _____   Cash Generation _____

Business _____   Selective Investment _____

Program _____   Growth_____

Unit No. _____

	Last Year	This Year	Plan Year 1
INCOME STATEMENT			
Revenue Dollars			
Trade sales			
Other income			
Total cost of sales			
Selling, marketing, and advertising			
Local and regional administrative			
Business unit and divisional co. administration			
R&D expense			
Corporate interest			
Excess cost amortization			
Earnings before income tax			
Average assets employed			
Return on investment			
Balance Sheet			
Cash			
Temporary investments			
Accounts receivable (net)			
Inventory			
Other current assets			
Property and facilities—net			
Investment in Non-Con. subs and affiliated co.			
Long-term trade receivables and other assets			
Excess of cost over net assets acquired			
Notes payable			
Accounts payable—trade			
Current maturities of long-term debt			
Current income tax liability			
Other current liabilities			
Long-term debt (net of current portion)			
Deferred income tax			
Pension and other noncurrent amounts			
Equity or current account			
Total liabilities and equity			

business units had planned to distribute its new committed expenditures in the following manner: 10 percent, contraction; 35 percent, maintenance; 30 percent, replacement; and 25 percent, new venture projects. The expenditures necessary to implement these strategic action plans were developed from over 100 operational plans which ranged from simply meeting EPA and OSHA requirements to replacing worn-out equipment, increasing market share, and entering new markets. This kind of planning allowed management to determine the funds necessary to continue, improve, shrink, or expand each business area, given the product life cycle and competitive position. On the basis of these findings, internal negotiations are instituted with strategies, expenditures, and goals agreed upon.

A one-page summary containing the following condensed data dealing with all the planning years is also drawn up. These figures and ratios help management notice any inconsistency within its plans and financial structure.

Net income
Sales
Change in sales
Total capital employed
Sales per dollar of expense
Receivables and change
Inventories and change
Plant, property, and equipment
Capital expenditures
Orders received
Number of full-time employees
Sales per employee
Number of full-time salesmen
Sales per salesman
Net income per employee

Percentage return on sales
Percentage return on assets
Percentage return/capital employed
Percentage credit sales to net sales
Percentage receivables to sales
Percentage new investments to sales
Advertising and promotion expenditures
Percentage advertising and promotion to sales
Change in capital ratios

GOVERNMENT MARKETS

With the stroke of the pen, the people down in Washington can take away ten years of effort. It's no use trying to do anything with a business that Washington won't let you do.

—JOHN E. SWEARINGEN
Chairman and Chief Executive Officer
Standard Oil Company (Indiana)

The immensity of the government and its involvement in our daily existence requires that you as a manager consider that at some point in your business life cycle it may become necessary for you to do business with Uncle Sam. If appropriately planned, your participation need not be perilous. The most important aspect for success is to know what is expected of you.

Your involvement with the behemoth that is the U.S. government—with its necessarily compartmentalized, decentralized, and often conflicting activities—makes it difficult to understand the total process, which may result in events that shake the very foundation of your corporate existence. (Recall the cases of Lockheed, Pan Am, Penn Central, General Dynamics, and Litton Industries.) With proper planning, you can prepare for success and survival in this seemingly unfathomable, hierarchical maze of people, projects, and programs.

In this section, it is not our intention to teach you how to win government contracts. We will note some pitfalls you will encounter that must be included in your decision process if you intend to win government contracts or are currently involved in doing so. Past multi-industry experience has demonstrated that to be effective and successful with government business, a manager needs to be aware of the risks and, more important, cognizant of the costs that must be controlled. In general, the cost process goes according to the following scenario:[5]

Should Cost
Will Cost
Must Cost

Incentives exist for procurement officers to establish the most favorable contract negotiating positions on the basis of the officer's concept of what a system *should cost.* This appears to contradict incentives to establish, for resource allocation purposes, the best estimate of what a system *will cost.* Confounding the cost estimating problem is the incentive for all participants to establish those costs necessary to remain in contention for limited resources, such resources being what the system *must cost.*

The winner of the battle of cost-estimating philosophies is *must cost.* This highly competitive environment of one buyer and many sellers is dedicated to the proposition that costs must be lower. Remember, living with a *must cost* number is not unlike living on the side of a volcano: one may live in peace and tranquility for years without getting burned, although that peril is always present. Our only advice on this subject is to make certain that you know your three cost figures before entering the bid process. If you ignore a high *will cost* to reach what you perceive the contract *must cost,* you are likely to be in trouble. For further advice, we suggest that you read "Unmanned Space Project Management," a NASA publication by Erasmus H. Kloman, which has extensive discussions of actual case histories.

To conduct business profitably in this environment, entry into the government contracting arena must be carefully planned, with potential impacts to operations identified, analyzed, and under-

[5] Wayne M. Allen, "A Theory on the Cause of Cost Growth," *Procurement Association,* August 1963.

stood. As we have discussed earlier in this book, in any business activity a thorough understanding of one's potential customers and market is essential to success. In government marketing this understanding is difficult to achieve as a result of the inherent complexities in dealing with a large bureaucratic system, and the proliferation of regulations under which agencies are required to conduct business with private industry. Qualifying, reporting requirements, coordination with various agencies, assigning responsibilities to ensure compliance, and performance of contract terms and conditions will require an extensive commitment of your resources to ensure a reasonable degree of success. If you do not have your own staff trained for government procedures, you will need to hire a specialist consultant to help you.

Among key matters to observe in successfully doing business with various government agencies are cost accounting standards; performance measurement requirements; requirements of government contracts; and contract close-out.

Cost Accounting Standards

In recent years, one of the more significant requirements affecting an enterprise doing business with government agencies has been the establishment of cost accounting standards. These standards, rules, and regulations promulgated pursuant to 50 U.S.C. App. 2168 (Public Law 91–379, August 15, 1970) require a contractor to disclose his accounting practices and to comply with cost accounting standards as established by the Cost Accounting Standard Board.

The impact of these standards is potentially far-reaching on the management and financial systems of an enterprise contemplating doing business with the U.S. government. For this reason, a thorough understanding of their implications should be achieved in evaluating and planning an entry into the government contracting arena. An initial step toward this understanding of cost accounting standards and other government contracting requirements can be obtained through a review of the Armed Services Procurement Regulations, which serve as a model for other government agencies.

Performance Measurement Requirements

Any system used by the contractor in planning and control must comply with government standards. The Department of Defense's requirements are typical in stating that "contractors' internal management control systems must provide data which (a) indicate work progress; (b) properly relate cost, schedule, and technical accomplishment; (c) are valid, timely, and auditable; and (d) supply DOD managers with information at a practicable level of summarization . . . DOD contractors also should be continuously alert to advances in management control systems which will improve their internal operations."

Detailed procedures are in the *Cost Schedule Control Systems Criteria Joint Implementation Guide.* The DOD will regularly review the contractor's systems to be sure that they are in compliance, and that they continue to fairly reflect the proper assignment of costs.

Requirements of Government Contracts

The contractor is faced with an overwhelming array of forms that must be filled out correctly and on time. If you do not have the in-house experience to do this, you must hire a specialist to guide you through the maze of forms required by the agency with which you are dealing. Try to remember that the forms are designed by earnest and generally competent people who are trying to get better performance from contractors for the benefit of their agencies and the taxpayers. The forms are designed for the "typical" contract. But since there is no such thing as a "typical" contract, it will be difficult to understand how the forms apply to your particular contract.

Contract Close-Out

This involves getting paid, making any final adjustments, being sure that all the paperwork is completed correctly so that items will not come back to haunt you later, and maintaining good relations with agency personnel so that you will have a better chance to get the next contract. Again, if you do not have the in-house experience, you must use the outside specialist you have hired to help you work through this final, but vital, part of the contract.

It is not always easy. Recently, the U.S. Navy has been at odds with American shipbuilders: General Dynamics has even threatened to cease working on nuclear submarines despite its contract to deliver. (Delivery of 16 submarines still to be built is currently running up to 3½ years behind schedule.) Pentagon officials are concerned about the long-term defense and procurement impacts of this dispute in which General Dynamics could potentially lose over $800 million on the original $1.8 billion contract. The company and the Navy blame each other for the problem. General Dynamics charges that the government has made more than 35,000 changes in the designs and plans for the subs since the company started work on them in 1970. These changes are occurring at a rate of 200 to 300 a week! Partly for this reason, it took the company 7.1 million man-hours to build the first sub, compared with the 3.8 million man-hours that General Dynamics had originally planned. Obviously, dealing with the government is no simple task and can be risky.

To conclude this discussion, let us quote from Grant E. Williams, Manager of Administrative Services at Martin Marietta Corporation, who has had extensive dealings with government agencies as a consultant and as a member of a large corporate contractor. "Effective long-range planning by industry assumes effective interagency coordination and overall planning by the government," he says. "To the degree that this coordination and planning by the government is ineffective, industry will incur needless expense resulting in an inappropriate expenditure of public funds."

To summarize, these are the stages you should go through in doing business as a government contractor:

1. When you win the job, know fully what your costs must be.
2. Show technical competence in performing the task.
3. Forms must be completed and submitted properly. (Some contractors feel this is their greatest challenge.)

HOW DO YOU KNOW WHEN YOU HAVE ARRIVED?

Like everything in life, there is a beginning and an end. Yet most planning systems concentrate on the beginning and not on the end. This doesn't seem unreasonable, given the investment of time and manpower in implementing a good planning system. For example, it took both GE and Mead over four years to plan, equip, and implement their system. So it is not surprising that an important question sometimes gets overlooked: "Have I arrived?"

Since all strategic or action plans are directed toward goals and these goals support the corporation's objectives, it is fitting that all results be measured against the goals that were formulated early in the planning cycles. We realize that this is sometimes difficult. For example, we know of a refinery that was built in the late 1960s, which served only as reserve capacity. Management later changed this facility's goal to one of increasing sales with a minimum increase in the labor force. After the oil embargo of 1973, sales increased dramatically in price and volume with limited increases in the labor force (although additions to the labor force were somewhat greater than planned). As a result, the plant reached capacity quickly, and a new goal of a second facility was formulated to meet the new demand.

The planning process may also cause a revision of corporate goals. If, after a specific time span with reasonable targets, a goal is not reached, then either the goal has to be modified or the action plan was incorrect in the first place. For example, we were involved in a joint venture with some Middle Eastern governments to develop a consumer market for some of their locally produced products. After four years, growth did not materialize as planned. The planning process, though, has enabled the partners to determine what is now feasible in light of how far away they are from their goal, as indicated by the new information.

The key to performance is the ability to meet your specific goals. The planning process provides a roadmap to minimize the problems in obtaining these goals. It gives management insight and performance criteria to understand the dynamics in meeting management goals.

Finally, start again! The planning process is self-regenerative. Contrary to what you may feel, the process does not end with the generation of a plan; this step is merely the starting point for performing, measuring, adjusting, and restarting. Any successful plan must have measurable milestones. Seldom have we found companies who measure performance on any basis other than a one-year horizon. Each plan should be compared with its predecessors to assess its total performance, and each should have the flexibility to change its structure. Remember, periodic checkups allow for responses to change *before* a catastrophe occurs.

SOURCE LIST

The Future

The Futurist
> Interesting but uneven magazine that will surely give you some interesting thoughts to ponder.

Yankelovitch Monitor
Harris Poll
Gallup Poll
University of Michigan Survey
> These polling groups offer worthwhile insights into current beliefs and opinions of the U.S. population and various segments, along with trend information that can be invaluable for making predictions about future values and reactions.

Technology Assessment
> Covers changing technology as well as guidance in keeping track of technological changes and determining what they mean to you and your business.

National Science Foundation
NASA Research Reports
> NSA annually and NASA about 25 times per year summarize research done. Give worthwhile ideas on areas of current interest and future trends.

Government Data Publications*
> *Contracts Monthly* and *The Research & Development Directory* report on government contracts by agency, type of research, and company. Along with information on new technology, you may get some knowledge of what your competitors are doing and some ideas for applying research being paid for by the government.

American Demographics
P.O. Box 68
Ithaca, N.Y. 14850
> This is a new magazine that applies census and other demographic information to the kinds of forecasts that are needed for business purposes.

---

* All government publications are available from the Superintendent of Documents, Government Printing Office, Washington, D.C. 20402.

The Economy

U.S. Department of Commerce
Bureau of the Census
Statistical Abstract of the U.S. is an annual report on everything you could possibly want to know about the population, housing, incomes, prices, international trade, and the like. The 1980 Census began on April 1, 1980. The wealth of data flowing from the census became available starting in autumn 1980 for preliminary population and housing data broken down to the city and county level. Details down to the block level will be available in the first half of 1981. The census will tell you everything you need to know about the demographics of the American people and their homes. Meanwhile *Current Population Reports* gives estimates and projections.

Council of Economic Advisors
Monthly Economic Indicators and the *Annual Report* contain a wealth of economic statistics.

Federal Reserve Banks
All regional banks have monthly bulletins full of economic statistics (usually too abstruse for noneconomists) and equally technical articles.

National and regional banks
Most have monthly economic and business newsletters. Among the better ones are those of Morgan Guaranty and Bankers Trust in New York. Available on request.

General Business

The Conference Board
845 Third Avenue
New York, N.Y. 10022
Many publications on business with many special research reports on management topics including economic conditions, finance, and international business.

U.S. Department of Commerce
Office of Business Economics
Survey of Current Business covers monthly data on many economic and business indicators including prices, production, income, employment, orders, shipments, and some generalized industry data.

Bureau of the Census
Census of Manufacturers (latest covers 1975 data) offers summaries of past data on many industries (to four-digit SIC code) including employment, production, shipments, sources of materials and energy. *Survey of Manufacturers* gives the same information yearly, but only to two-digit SIC code.

Bureau of Economic Analysis
Business Conditions Digest gives national aggregated income, production, and similar information on a monthly basis.

Bureau of Labor Statistics
Statistical Summary is a monthly report on employment by industry, wages, production, and so forth.

U.S. Department of the Interior
Bureau of Mines
Minerals Yearbook gives worldwide production data for minerals, metals, and fuel. *Geological Survey* covers water supply and some other minerals. Vital if your business is dependent on these raw material resources.

Department of Agriculture
Agricultural Abstract gives annual crop reports and forecasts. Again, vital if your business depends on agricultural raw materials.

Federal Power Commission
Annual statistical books give capacity, output, operating, and financial data on utilities. Useful if power supply is critical, but usually you can get a better picture for your own needs by talking to executives of your local utilities or the public service commissions in the states where you operate.

Your Industry

Industry associations
Industry journals
Industry newsletters
The associations and publications in your particular industry are likely to be the best sources of information on what is happening and what is likely to happen in your industry, what your competitors around the world are up to, changes in technology, and so forth.

It is also worthwhile to attend industry meetings. If the association in your industry is not helpful, either get on the board of directors and improve it, or form a new industry association.

U.S. Department of Commerce

Bureau of the Census
Industry Profiles census tape gives information on employees, wages, productivity, costs, capital investment, inventories, and so forth, to four-digit SIC codes, which is fairly general.

Specialized research organizations such as:
Predicasts, Inc.
Frost & Sullivan, Inc.
Morton Research
Noyes Development (chemicals)
Charles H. Kline & Co. (chemicals)
International Resource Development, Inc.
Business Communications Co.

These organizations do extensive studies of industries, usually with considerable information on the leading companies, technological developments, key factors, trends, and the like. They are expensive, but worthwhile if they cover your particular industry. Write them for catalogs of available reports. Predicasts, Inc. also publishes the *Technical Survey* of abstracts from general and technical publications worldwide. Available in print and as a computer data base.

Your Competition

Annual reports and 10K reports
Usually provided free on request. 10K reports, required by the SEC, are more detailed and are broken down by main lines of business. Most companies are adept at being misleading in both reports.

Moody's
Standard & Poor's
Their manuals have summaries and current information on all publicly held companies.

Value Line
Provides short summaries and stock price information on all publicly held companies.

Dun & Bradstreet
> *Million Dollar Directory, Middle Market Directory,* and *Metal Working Directory* give brief information about company location, product lines, sales, employee number, and senior management. Credit reports on individual companies are available to subscribers. These are expensive and not of much use except for credit purposes.

Barron's
Wall Street Transcript
> Carry reports on analysts' meetings, top management speeches, and similar information. *Barron's* occasionally comes through with excellent industry studies.

Fortune
Forbes
> Both magazines have directories showing comparative performance of major companies. *Forbes* tends to group by industry, *Fortune* by size of the firm. Both often have useful articles on particular companies.

General Information

Library
> Your company library or local library may have a good business section. The index of periodicals lists articles by subject, making it relatively easy for you to find the industry, company, or management problems that you are concerned with, as well as to find out what has been written on the subject recently. Getting the articles may be difficult if you do not have a good library, and may require contacting the publications office.

FIND/SVP
500 Fifth Avenue
New York, N.Y. 10036
> If you cannot find an article, or enough information on a subject, FIND can. Through its computer terminals, it has access to 300 computerized data banks, many of them highly specialized by industry. The staff can also do library searches for what your library does not have. This service is available on an annual subscription basis and will probably cost a minimum of $150 per month. FIND also has company (and some industry) studies prepared by specialized research groups and by Wall Street investment houses for their

clients. These studies may be out of date for investment purposes, but are valuable for company and industry background. They cost from $50 to $2,500 apiece.

Washington Researchers
918 16th St., N.W.
Washington D.C. 20006

Units of the federal government are always doing studies and holding hearings, many of them on industries in which you should be interested. This information is hard to find, but Washington Researchers can find it for you or train you to find it yourself. Again, it's expensive but worth it.

Starch Reports
W.R. Simmonds
Target Group Index
Market Facts
A.C. Nielsen
S.A.M.I.
Towne Oller Trends

All of these services give information on competitors' performance in consumer markets in a variety of forms. They are expensive, and whether they are worth it will depend on your particular industry and your own needs.

International Business

United Nations Publishing Service
One Dag Hammarskjold Plaza
New York, N.Y. 10017

Statistical Yearbook gives vast amounts of data on each member country, with varying degrees of reliability. *Yearbook of International Trade Statistics* covers imports and exports by SITC code.

Office of Economic Cooperation and Development
OECD Publication Center
1750 Pennsylvania Ave.
Washington, D.C. 20006

Economic Outlook is a monthly publication that provides detailed statistical studies of member countries. *Foreign Trade Statistics Bulletins* cover trade among members.

International Labor Office
  Yearbook of Labor Statistics covers labor and price data for most countries. Its reliability is variable.

U.S. Department of Commerce
  Bureau of International Commerce
  Overseas Business Reports comes out 40–50 times per year. It covers economics, business trends and opportunities, market characteristics, and regulations in foreign countries.
  Foreign Economic Trends, published with equal frequency, contains reports from foreign trade counsels. The value varies with the skills of the particular counsel.
  Business America covers export opportunities and problems fortnightly.
  Foreign Traders Index is a computer data base listing 150,000 firms in 130 countries for trade contacts.

Business International
One Dag Hammarskjold Plaza
New York, N.Y. 10017
  The leading private information source for international business. Publishes numerous periodicals and special reports, which are exceptionally useful and moderately priced. Seminars, roundtables in foreign countries, and numerous special reports and services are available to clients at higher costs. Any company seriously interested in international markets should be a client of Business International. If you think the price is too high, stick to your domestic market.

4

PLANNING — Business Style (Part 2)

It is only when strategic planning is integrated with strong action programs and wise investment decisions that its value is realized by the corporation. —E. M. DEWINDT
Chairman and CEO
Eaton Corporation

Companies have begun to change their perspectives on planning the future. As the environment has shifted from one of unparalleled growth to one of limited resources with obscured opportunities, companies are discovering the contribution planning can make. The following sections present current state-of-the-art planning practices in several large, medium-size, and small companies across the industrial spectrum. Whether or not these planning systems (or portions thereof) fit your environment is a question you must answer for your own company.

THE CASE OF PULLMAN, INC.: A COMPANY THAT CHANGED DIRECTION

Before presenting examples of strategic planning, we felt it would be worthwhile to first discuss how and why a company moves toward strategic planning. We were seeking an example of a company that completely changed its business focus. In reviewing industries and companies that experienced dramatic environmental shifts which necessitated change, one company stood out—Pullman, Inc. Most people view Pullman as a railroad car manufacturer. In fact, although the company is the largest manufacturer of railroad equipment in the Free World, this area comprises less than 30 percent of Pullman's business. Today, Pullman's thrust is in the design and construction of chemical and petroleum facilities as well as steel plants and furnaces, where it is considered a world leader in both design and construction technology. This change was the result of a strategic assessment of the company in 1970 by its then newly appointed chairman, Samuel B. Casey, Jr. The following excerpts from the authors' in-depth interview with this chief executive in 1978 highlight the significant points in our case for strategic thinking.

QUESTION: Mr. Casey, under your direction Pullman has changed its strategic thrust. The following quote is attributed to you: "I made a commitment that I would run Pullman, during my tenure, dedicated to strategic planning. Pullman would pick its road." What led you to this conclusion?

ANSWER: Getting back to the old chestnut, "Do times make the man or does man make the time?," I was shocked and disappointed when I arrived here in 1970 to discover that Pullman had no formal planning process or written documents to which I could refer to determine in what directions my predecessor was leaning. I asked for these plans, but none were here. I decided to institute a formal planning process as soon as possible—which was done in 1971. . . . Getting back to the little chestnut about times making the man or man making the times . . . , in 1971, the largest U.S. railroad, the Penn Central, was going bankrupt. Did that have an effect on my thinking? That answer unquestionably was "yes," in view of the demands on my time and thoughts. Beyond this occurrence, the Yom Kippur War in November 1973 had a remarkable effect on the contemplative managers of America. If it didn't—and if it didn't change their life radically—something was wrong. Perhaps they should have gone into the priesthood rather than running a multinational company.

Those two events were telltale signs that had to have a marked effect on our markets, our business planning, and strategic planning. And they did! The emphasis we have placed on our planning was *survival*. For Pullman, it was fortunate to have a person who enjoys problems (due to my engineering and construction background) to act as Horatio on the bridge. We have really taken great advantage of the construction and engineering personnel, available dollars, and available organizations. I had an excellent base from which to build and took rather big risks, which have paid off!

QUESTION: Mr. Casey, how much of your time is devoted to strategic thinking? Secondly, how much time do you think your divisional presidents allocate to strategic planning?

ANSWER: A quick response is—less than it should be. The longer answer is that as the years go on, I find the amount of time increasing. I would say that at least 50 percent of my time is devoted to planning; a truly ideal time portion would be 80 percent.

As for the division presidents, I think individually they spend more time on planning, or at least as much as I do. To guess at the trend, I am certain each divisional president will spend twice the amount of time devoted to planning as he did two years ago. I think that, with the commonality of all divisions, this is a correct statement.

On second thought, getting back to my personal involvement, I probably devote more than 50 percent of my time to strategic thinking if I include government and regulatory affairs.

QUESTION: Mr. Casey, Pullman has now had a formal planning process since 1971. How would you view its acceptance throughout the organization by the line operating managers?

ANSWER: Let me clarify one thing: we don't have one divisional president who really enjoys anything about planning. Planning is work, it is tough, perhaps it's the toughest thing that happens in the day. There is no immediate fallout from your effort; you've got to wait and wait and wait. As a matter of fact, I am concerned about the future when some of our divisional people approach retirement. Will they continue to plan at the age of 63 or 64? They're all professional enough to know there is a long gestation period when the health of the baby at birth is unknown.

QUESTION: What is the structure of your planning efforts?

ANSWER: If the planning function isn't reporting to the chief executive officer, emphasis is not being placed in the appropriate places. I can also say something else, and it's very unpopular: if the person in charge of government relations is not reporting to the chief executive officer, that company knows little about America or where America is heading. I would have to conclude that those company managers don't know how to run their businesses.

QUESTION: Who develops the objectives and what time horizon does your planning process cover?

ANSWER: Initially, I had a pretty clear idea about the kind of company I wanted to leave in 1980. Since I sat on the board for three or four years before my election as chief executive, I had a rough idea of the type of company I was inheriting. In the early part of 1971, when we formalized the planning process, I communicated my intentions to the divisional operating people. As part of the formalization process, all corporate officers were involved in a Pullman self- and market-analysis. What kind of company was Pullman? What did we think we could be? What kinds of problems did we see? What were the opportunities?

It took a while, but a consensus developed. The objectives are really authored by the divisions. They determine directions and programs. Corporate management reserves the right to modify these objectives. So what really happens is that we end up with a consensus objective.

As to planning horizons, it depends on the individual business area. Some of the technological horizons in our divisions are out 12 or 15 years. Some of the product development systems are out seven years. Some of the other systems are out three or four years. For convenience of pulling it together and making it make sense, our strategic plan right now runs out seven years. There's nothing magical about the number of years; all we wanted to do was run the horizon out far enough so that an intelligent guy could not say to us without thinking, "It's going to look in 1985 just the way it does now." We simply set the horizon far enough so that if indeed change is likely, he's going to think about it and he's going to talk about it and we can interact on how we are going to respond to the change.

QUESTION: Could you be a bit more specific?

ANSWER: Let me now put a little bit of "where we have been" into the perspective of the decade of the 1970s, and also "where we are planning to be" in the decade of the 1980s.

I am now almost eight years into my tenure, and I have kept my commitment to strategic planning. We are on the verge of completing an extensive and comprehensive strategic planning project we fondly refer to as "Strat Plan II." It is our blueprint as to how we will complete Pullman's transition from a collection of almost unrelated companies (circa 1970) to a corporation that has a cohesive concept and interrelated pieces (circa 1978).

Let me share with you some of the concepts in Strat Plan II.

First, let's describe our commitment to what Pullman stands for: Pullman's overall objective is to be regarded as a "great" company. In a nutshell, it means to us that when knowledgeable people— those that are the true "influence centers" in the investment and financial community—are asked to name the great companies, Pullman will be included on that list; and that we must effectively relate to our "public" on the terms that they establish. Several of Pullman's most important publics are its:

Customers. Accordingly, we have adopted a clear-cut dedication that Pullman will serve their true needs.

Shareholders. Accordingly, we will ensure Pullman's ability to perceive and meet the performance criteria that they establish.

Employees (who make up the really valuable assets). Accordingly, we will ensure our ability to meet their aspirations.

Others (who are affected or influenced by our firm). We will recognize and meet their legitimate needs.

A second conclusion from Strat Plan II deals with Pullman's business concept and its management style. First, Pullman intends to develop itself around a cohesive business concept. So that it can understand its businesses and be understood, we intend to serve, on a worldwide basis, five major industry/market "sectors." These sectors are as follows: transportation, materials handling, energy, chemicals, and natural resources.

This is Pullman's "to whom we serve":

> We intend to serve these "sectors" by providing tangible products, finance and leasing services, project management services, and after-market services.

This is Pullman's "with what we offer":

> We have synthesized a concept, by combining the "what" and "who" into a "matrix." Our "concept" is that Pullman's business is "transporting and transforming material."

In a nutshell, Pullman relates to *material*, whether it be transportation equipment; a role of transporting materials; materials handling equipment; the sources of solid and liquid energy; sources and facilities for energy and chemical conversion; or the extraction, processing, transportation, and transformation of natural resources.

Secondly, let's discuss management style. Pullman is committed to a concept of well-defined decentralization. It is a simple concept of delegated authority and of concurrent accountability.

Third, we have a concept of business balance. To us, our concept of balance is pervasive. It means balance in growth, in resource consumption, resource generation, geographies, types of businesses, the risk/reward, and so forth.

A final conclusion of Strat Plan II deals with our financial objectives. Strat Plan II sets forth specific financial objectives upon which I prefer not to elaborate.

QUESTION: Mr. Casey, how do you view the planning individual?

ANSWER: I look at the planning discipline as being key to corporate survival. In reality, participation in the formal planning function is a necessary ingredient in a manager's development, although it should be short in duration—perhaps three or four years. Let me reiterate: planners and operating managers must have close communications and constant interaction. It is from situations such as these that opportunities are identified.

With this insight into a chief executive's thought process, we will now discuss some formal planning systems. These are divided into three categories: large multinationals, medium-size corporations, and small companies.

LARGE MULTINATIONAL CORPORATIONS: INTERNATIONAL BUSINESS MACHINES

IBM initiates its planning process through the development of formal statements of strategic direction for each industry it serves. These are prepared by both the American and foreign marketing organizations in conjunction with the appropriate product development divisions. These statements emphasize the articulation of customer needs along with the identification of the product and marketing actions necessary to meet these needs on a multinational basis.

Key to this process is constant study and analysis of the customer business environment to understand customer goals, the necessary customer strategies to achieve these, and needed data processing capabilities. In addition to direct customer contact, information is collected from government and research organizations. Data availability is enhanced through computer access to cross-reference data bases and the use of computer models. Special emphasis is placed on the definition of implementation programs for each industry strategic direction. This definition, provided in conjunction with the formal strategy statements, helps keep planning and marketing functions synchronized, and is a direct input to operating plan commitments.

Origin of IBM's Business Systems Planning Function

Learning from its own mistakes and from those of other companies that attempted to implement large information systems in the 1960s, IBM realized that a disciplined approach was required, using proven principles and methods. In 1966, a businesswide information systems control and planning department was established at IBM's data processing group headquarters. The data processing group was a total business unit comprising the engineering, manufacturing, sales, and service divisions responsible for all of IBM's domestic data processing business.

Until the control and planning department was established, IBM had little overall direction for the internal use of computers and the initial coordination of the plan. In fact, little coordination of any sort took place between divisions; most activities were confined to locations and units within divisions. Consequently, each manufacturing plant and marketing region developed and operated its own system. Although the individual systems carried out similar functions, they differed in design and performance: they could not be used interchangeably and could not communicate with each other. The result was a redundancy of data and excessive use of the data processing resources required to develop and maintain many such systems. Even with this large expenditure of resources by each division, the systems were mainly satisfying local department needs rather than doing an overall data processing job. Worse, by the end of the 1950s, they were competing with each other.

For instance, the IBM 1401 series was handled by the General Products Division in Endicott, New York. The 1401 was a highly successful small business computer that generated about two thirds of IBM's sales, and was expected to satisfy the market through 1968. At the same time, the 7000 series was handled by the Data Systems Division in Poughkeepsie, New York. The 7000 series of large computers was surpassed in both performance and capacity by the 7090 scientific computer. At the top of the line, the Data Systems Division was working on its huge STRETCH computer. In the middle range, the smaller computers in the 7000 line and the larger ones in the 1401 line were beginning to compete directly.

By 1959, IBM management was concerned with the internal competition of the two lines; with the tremendous costs and difficulties of supporting and servicing the many computers in the line (each of which had its own program, connection, and servicing requirements); and with the erosion by competitors of IBM's markets.

In 1961, the STRETCH computer was canceled, with a loss of about $20 million, because it was never able to achieve its design goals. Data Systems then proposed a new 8000 line, envisioning it to be a fast second-generation series that could be expected to stay on the market through 1968. By midyear, the 8000 series was rejected, and Data Systems recommended a 7000 series extension.

At this point, it was discovered that the Hurley Laboratory in London was developing a computer named "Scamp" with approximately the same characteristics as the 7044 being developed by Data Systems. A decision was made in favor of the 7044, and the London computer was scrapped. This offended World Trade Corp., which had tried three times to develop its own computers for the European market and had been turned down by IBM—its parent company—each time. It also started IBM's top management looking at new product development.

The company discovered that between 15 and 20 engineering groups were always working independently on different projects. The products they developed were generally good, but each had different characteristics and required a separate programming and support group. IBM was losing control of its new product development and of its support and programming activities. There were too many products in too many markets. Clearly, product design, development, production, and marketing would have to be coordinated on a companywide basis.

The first effort of the control and planning department was to inventory and profile the systems existing within the business, as well as the plans for the future. The group then defined a network of information systems and it assigned responsibilities for the development of the systems.

Significant conclusions were drawn that should not surprise any manager:

- Businesses should change in response to changes in their environment.
- The success of a business depends to a great extent on the effectiveness of management decisions.
- The effectiveness of management decisions is closely related to the information on which they are based.
- Resource optimization is a key to increased profitability.
- Management control is a key to resource optimization.
- Information systems requirements should be identified from the top down; design and implementation requirements should be identified from the bottom up.
- Because organizational changes generally occur more frequently than changes to business activities, information systems designed to support the business activities will survive longer and be easier to maintain.
- Management must apply leadership to achieve the desired output.

IBM believes that a basic framework is needed for approaching the subject of management planning and control systems. Usually, planning and control are discussed in theory as separate management functions. In practice, however, these are not separate activities carried on at different times or by different people. To be effective, planning and control must be integrated; furthermore, they must be integrated vertically to include the functions of strategic planning, management control, and operational control.

The planning team's first task was to gain a broad understanding of the business. The team identified the key elements necessary to analyze the information requirements of the business. Those key elements and their relationship are shown in Figure 7.

In its top-down analysis of the business and of the information necessary to support the business, the planning team first required a knowledge of the objectives identified by management and of the

Figure 7. Key elements in analyzing a business's information requirements.

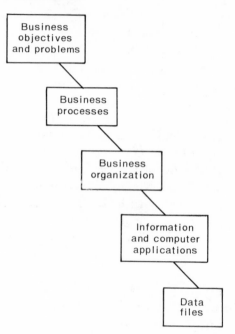

problems faced by the business in meeting those objectives. Certain processes must be performed by the business to enable it to meet its objectives; the planning team's second step was to identify those processes or define them when necessary. The team then related the current organization, with its assigned responsibilities and activities, to the various processes.

Management activities and decisions become more planning- and control-oriented at progressively higher levels of management. The framework for classifying management planning and control activity is as follows:

1. Strategic Planning
   Business: Goals and objectives, image, marketplace, product lines, ventures, acquisitions, organization, management system.

   Resources: Policy relative to personnel, facilities, material, vendors, customers.

   Financial: Targets and policy relative to revenue, expense, profit, ROI, investments, dividends.

2. Management Control
   Product: Definition, selection, forecasting, pricing, sales objectives, volumes, balancing of supply and demand.

   Resources: Requirements definition, allocation, and retirement decisions relative to resources.

   Financial: Budgeting, revenue-cost control, product-line profitability, productivity economics by product line, organization—growth- or cash-flow-oriented.

3. Operational Control
   Product: Design, make-or-buy, production, inventory, distribution, maintenance, sales, order-entry, advertising.

   Resources: Acquisition (recruitment, hiring, vendor analysis, purchasing) and use (record keeping on raw materials and product lines) of resources.

   Financial: Cost accounting, receivables, payables, billings, disbursements, payroll, general ledger.

The rapidly changing environment and the need for businesses to adjust quickly to these changes make it necessary for executive management to have useful information available when it is needed. The information should be structured and processed as an integrated system. It should give executives the ability to make meaningful resource allocation trade-offs. With a plan that leads to the implementation of information systems to support the processes of the business as a whole, such data can be more readily obtained.

Organizing for Planning

The planning and control system of IBM serves as a primary communication link between corporate and operating unit management for establishing unit objectives and strategic direction, negotiating plan commitments, and measuring performance against plan. The bulk of the planning done within IBM is not only decentralized and divided among several operating units, but planning within any given unit is further decentralized to the country, plant, and laboratory levels.

As we have said, planning and implementation are line management responsibilities. However, planning staffs to support line management exist at the corporate, operating unit (and, when these are large, at the divisional or country), and plant/laboratory levels. The size and functional mix of these staffs depend on the specific responsibilities of the line manager they support. At the operating unit level, the executive will normally have financial planning, as well as functional, skills needed to develop a properly balanced profit plan. For example, his technical staff will review and assist in integrating the various product plans into the unit plan. The unit executive makes the final judgments as to volumes to be achieved, resources required, and risks to be accepted.

At the corporate level, the line executives also have finance, planning, and other functional staffs to assist them. For example, among the responsibilities of the corporate business plans staff are design of the IBM planning system, establishing the plan guidance and data requirements, managing the plan schedule, recommending profit targets for the various operating units, and reviewing and assessing their strategies and plans.

Program and Period Planning

There are two distinct but interactive kinds of planning within the IBM system, as shown in Figure 8:

Program planning (such as a program to develop a product or improve the productivity of a function) is characterized by the following: the program plan generally has a single objective, but may involve several functional elements. Its time horizon is determined by the nature of the specific program objective and of the work processes required to achieve it; its cycle for review and decision making is determined by the inherent dynamics of the program. At any one time, each operating unit has a large portfolio of product and functional programs in various stages of planning and implementation.

Period planning complements program planning. The period plans balance among multiple program and other objectives to achieve the profit targets assigned. Its time horizons are fixed by corporate management, currently two years for the operating plan and five years for the strategic plan. The cycle for review and decision making is tied to the calendar to assure the availability of an operating budget for each unit at the beginning of each year.

Clearly, decisions made as part of the period planning process affect the program plans—accelerating some, terminating others, and so on. The converse is also true: some program decisions require changes in the period plan of an operating unit. It is the responsibility of operating unit management to establish and maintain the proper balance among its objectives and resources.

Application of the approach and methodology contained in IBM's planning system offers many potential benefits:

Top management communication and awareness
Agreed-upon priorities
A better long-range base for resources and funding

Figure 8. IBM period and program planning.

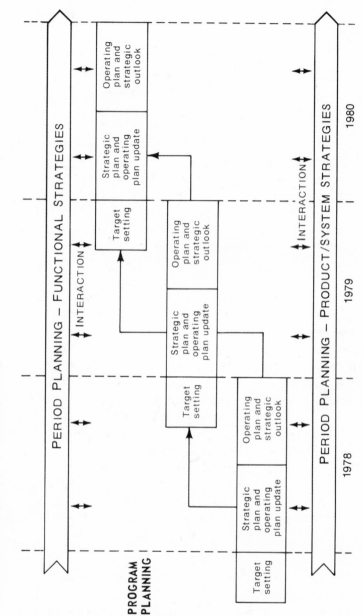

The plan that results from IBM's process is not considered immutable; it simply represents the best thinking at a certain time. The real value of the IBM approach is to create an environment and an initial plan of action that will enable a business to react to future changes in priorities and direction without radical disruptions in systems design.

LARGE MULTINATIONAL CORPORATIONS: GENERAL ELECTRIC

As General Electric has grown, the complexities brought about by increasing size and diversity have consistently challenged managers to develop new approaches, systems, and organization structures to meet the company's goals more effectively.

In the early 1950s, GE segmented its total business into a decentralized organization structure in which each building block—the department—had essentially the same growth objectives as the others. As expected, decentralization provided greater organizational flexibility and gave more people the opportunity to develop their managerial abilities. It encouraged managers to take a more entrepreneurial approach. As a consequence, decentralization was an important factor helping the company achieve strong growth during the favorable economic climate of the 1960s.

But that period also pointed out that growth in sales is not necessarily accompanied by a commensurate growth in earnings (see Figure 9). Investing in too many areas that did not yield profitable growth was an experience shared by many of the *Fortune 500* companies. This experience pointed up the need to be more selective in the allocation of resources.

The response of GE management was to introduce, in 1970, a strategic planning system. In essence, this system recognizes the need to differentiate among businesses. For a diversified company,

Figure 9. GE's pattern of profitless growth, 1962-1970.

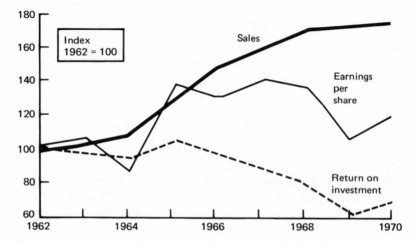

some operations can best serve by generating earnings, while others that have strong growth prospects offer better investment opportunities over the long term. This system gave GE the means to allocate resources according to the varying potentials of its many businesses.

Organizationally, on its traditional structure of groups, divisions, and departments, GE overlaid a structure for planning based on a new building block—the strategic business unit. SBUs were defined as self-contained businesses with identifiable external competitors and with general managers who could implement both long- and short-term business strategy. In addition, a planning process was designed by which each SBU submitted its strategic plans for review and resource allocation at the corporate level.

GE invested over four years in developing and implementing the system while continually updating the strategic planning process. In the 1970s, the system has helped GE improve its profitability and return on investment, and continues to adjust and improve the process as managers' planning experience grows and as the company adjusts to changes in the external environment.

At GE the planning process is not separated from the business processes. The basic thrust is not to have the plan developed by the strategic planning group, but rather to have it developed by the strategic business unit managers in conjunction with, and assisted by, the staff. The entire objective is to utilize both the strategic planning process and the resulting plan in the management of the business unit.

There were five main elements to the accomplishment of the planning development:

1. Some reorganization
2. A major staffing and training job
3. Establishment of a planning process
4. Development of tools to do the planning job at each level of the organization
5. Appropriate motivational systems development to put the planning into action

Figure 10 illustrates the time horizon under which GE introduced its strategic planning process.

GE believed that the ability to cope with business cycles is not an area where management often shines. When business is strong, the tendency is to assume that this condition will last. The same momentum syndrome works during periods when the economy is weak. As a result, the inclination is to manage within boundaries framed by shorter-term elements of euphoria or gloom. This "suboptimal" approach can be countered by stressing strategic portfolio priorities during any period when discontinuity from current trends is forecast for the economy. This allows a differentiated ap-

Figure 10. The introduction of GE's strategic planning process, 1970-1974.

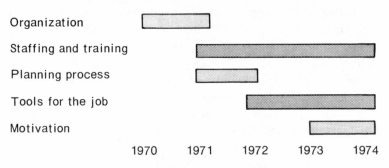

proach to possible cyclic changes rather than a less effective common response. In times when the economy is strong but when a downturn is anticipated, in addition to basic programs aimed at constraining overhead increases, key strategic programs should be accelerated even at the risk of imbalance or indigestion. These accelerations can be funded by a portion of the incremental profits available in boom times.. Strategic understanding allows acceleration of programs in segments where cost and market share benefits could be obtained by the time the economy declined.

Conversely when the economy is weak, but where the forecast is for recovery, the traditional tendency to squeeze every business uniformly is best resisted by a differentiated strategic approach that maintains growth projects and applies maximum pressure only in less attractive product or industry segments. The approach is summarized in Figure 11.

Basis of Planning

The business screen is used as the basis of GE's planning efforts, since it offers clues to a better understanding of the strategic busi-

Figure II. Action priorities for management at crucial points in the business cycle.

	Programs	Profits
Economy is **strong,** but **Downturn** is forecast	Accelerate or accept imbalance, indigestion	Use portion of incremental gains to position for cost and share improvement
Economy is **weak,** but **Improvement** is forecast	Preserve long-term projects	Squeeze weak product lines in less attractive industries

Figure 12. A typical business screen for an SBU ("Business X").

Industry Attractiveness	SBU Position
Profitability	
Leader has slight profit Balance breakeven or loss	GE breakeven in 1971; loss in 1970
Technical	
Patent constraints (short term) on Product B Patent questions on new Product E	GE Product B activity delayed May have to license
Other	
Environmental risk	Must monitor constantly — potential potential pollution impact, unique to GE
Industry operating at 50-70 percent capacity	GE at 54 percent in 1971

ness unit's competitive and strategic position. A typical SBU screen might look like the one shown in Figure 12. The next step is to position the unit on a competitive grid for each assessment factor, as in Figure 13. The last step is to build a competitive grid for the corporation as a whole (Figure 14).

Figure 13.   Positioning the unit on a competitive grid for each assessment factor.

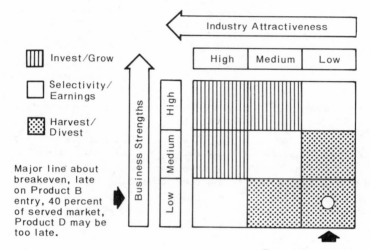

Everything wrong — over-
capacity, low profitability
foreign competition,
limited growth.

To complete the screen, GE's planners and managers seek information on the following areas:

1. Competitor information

    Domestic and foreign

    Existing, emerging, and potential

    Relative position in the industry

    Current and probable future strategies

    Strengths they will or can exploit

    Weaknesses or limitations GE can exploit, and vice versa

    Their unique problems and problems that GE shares with
        them

    Their motivations and likely behavior and posture

Figure 14. Building a competitive grid for the corporation as a whole (multidimensional portfolio assessment).

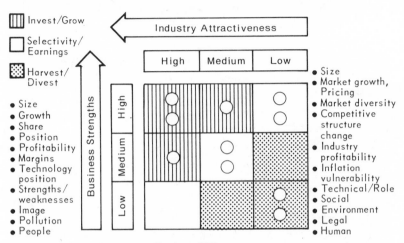

Each circle designates a distinct SBU.

Their capacity to react, and the likely direction of their
   reaction

What they will do next—on their own or as reactions to
   GE

2. Customer information

The small percentage who give GE the largest share of its
   sales

Their needs—real and imagined, product and service

Understanding of their end-use products and ultimate
   customers

Where their businesses are heading

Decision influence points, channels, and personnel

GE's historic ability to influence

   Why GE has been successful with them in the past and its
    likely ability to be so in the future
   What motivates their behavior
   Which are the most vulnerable to which competitors and
    why
   The major unserved customers and what it would take to
    crack that market
  3. Environmental factors
   Social, economic, political, and government trends—do-
    mestic and foreign
   Short-range probabilities and long-term trends
   Likely legislation—national and local
   Impact on customers and competitors
   Impact on this business
   GE's ability to influence these trends
   GE's ability to take advantage of these trends vs. the
    competition
   Pressures for change

Technology Planning

The business screen used as the basis of GE's planning efforts offers
the clue to a better understanding of the role of technology. In its
weaker businesses in less attractive industries (to the right of the di-
agonal in Figure 15), technology needs to provide "home runs"
that can favorably change a business equation and thus overcome
an industry weakness. In GE's stronger businesses in more attractive industries (see upper left of figure) the role of technology is different. Here, it must be targeted at any gaps that exist in the business to further strengthen solid competitive positions. Achieving
this result leads to great multiplication of business profit potential,
because successful technical programs are leveraged by high market shares.

  Regarding another important problem analysis of the impact

Figure 15. Business screen shows different roles of technology in GE's stronger and weaker businesses.

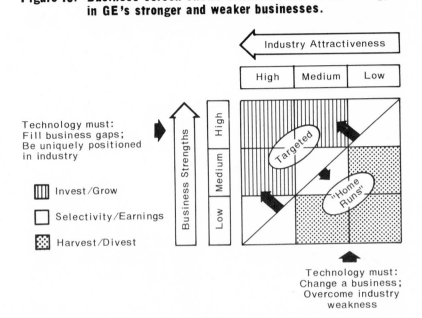

of inflation on another typical large company during the 1967–1972 period clearly pointed out its dramatic erosion effect on profitability. Nowhere was this more pronounced than in the raw materials purchasing area, where $35 million of five-year improvement in materials productivity was offset by a $30 million adverse materials price escalation effort. The net result was a modest favorable improvement in period dollar profits; but overall, there was an uneasy and precarious materials cost balance that could easily tip the wrong way in the future, as shown in Figure 16.

One way that a company in this situation would be able to hedge against severe price fluctuations is to use the commodities futures markets to "lock in" a price for copper, silver, and other valuable materials. When certain companies began this procedure

Figure 16. Materials cost balance: pretax effect of inflation on profits of a typical large company, 1967-1972.

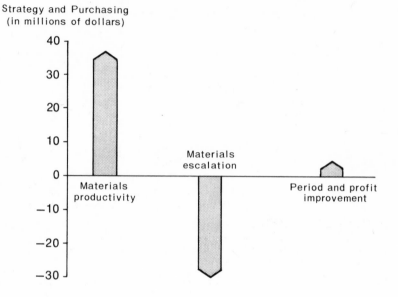

Strategy and Purchasing
(in millions of dollars)

several years ago, these metals were widely forecast to rise in price because of an upturn in world economy, tightening supply/demand equations, monetary and political uncertainties, and new needs for pollution control investments by producers. A typical example of hedging approaches implemented or under investigation by various multimillion-dollar corporations is shown in Figure 17.

Strategy and Management of Investment

In attempting to improve the management of investment, a common practice directs attention at aggregate dollars of fixed assets

Figure 17. Some hedging methods for price protection.

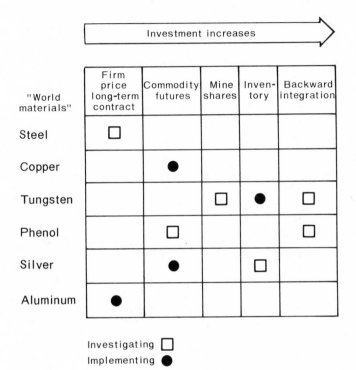

"World materials"	Firm price long-term contract	Commodity futures	Mine shares	Inven- tory	Backward integration
Steel	□				
Copper		●			
Tungsten			□	●	□
Phenol		□			□
Silver		●		□	
Aluminum	●				

Investigating □
Implementing ●

or working capital. Strategic analysis and related financial modeling in one GE group has developed the insight that it is the leverage equation that counts most. In this group, a ±5 percent change in the level of working capital tied up in inventories changes investment almost dollar for dollar (±4 percent), but a comparable percentage in market share or contribution margin yields a much more significant impact on investment (±19 percent in the first case, ±21 percent in the second). Thus, the perspective gained is to manage levels of inventories and receivables in a manner that will have the greatest impact on market share or contribution margin, or both, and not just to economize on current assets.

Planning and Incentive Compensation

Once a business mission is categorized in the group's portfolio, a sharper insight develops of the key characteristics required for the manager of that business. Matching the right person to the right business can accelerate that individual's own development and effectiveness. When designing compensation schemes for this person/business match, the mix of current results and future benefit

Figure 18. Designing compensation schemes in businesses at different stages of the growth cycle.

Basis of Compensation:

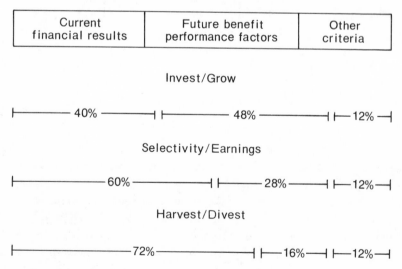

programs can be used as the key determinant in allocating incentive compensation (Figure 18). Entrepreneurial management efforts directed at future benefits should weigh much more heavily in assessing performance in an invest/grow business than in a harvest business, where the short range is paramount and the future is often cloudy and gloomy.

In Figure 18, the basis for managers' incentive compensation is broken down into the types of businesses they are managing. Thus, a manager in a harvest business is not rewarded for growth but for cash generation; the opposite is true for a manager in a growth business.

This approach has resulted in a much better fit of compensation with the differing objectives of each business. Further, it has reinforced strategic planning and improved the climate for individual effort. Key managers are rewarded not on the glamour of their business, but on how they performed versus expectations, whether in a harvest or a growth situation.

The Future

The structure described here was developed in the early 1970s and has been in place for several years. The results show that it has worked (see Figure 19). GE is now taking significant steps to meet the challenges of the 1980s.

The highest organization and planning level continues to be the corporate executive office, which is composed of the chairman and two vice chairmen. The CEO is responsible for overall corporate leadership and direction.

The next level of management and planning is the sector, which represents a larger business or industry area composed of a number of SBUs with similar strategic challenges, based on such factors as markets, products, customers, or technologies. The six sectors that have been established are sufficiently broad in scope

Figure 19. GE's improved pattern of results, 1962-1978.

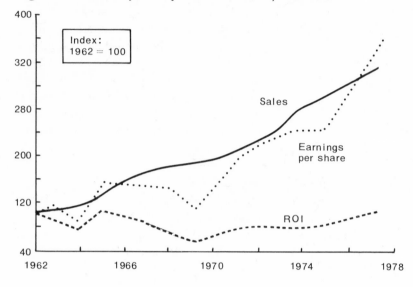

that the growth of the company is expected to take place within them for many years without the necessity for basic restructuring.

The sector provides a new level of strategy integration above the SBU. Thus, in addition to SBU plans, there will be sector plans and an overall corporate plan. Review of SBU plans at the sector level is expected to result in more comprehensive and meaningful attention applied to SBU strategies, resource allocation, and resource control, since the sector executive's portfolio of SBUs will be considerably smaller than those formerly reviewed by the vice chairmen.

The sector executive becomes GE's spokesman for his industries, allowing the CEO to concentrate to a greater extent on broad internal and external issues and the representation of the company as a whole. Below the sector level, the SBU continues to be the basic business entity. In many cases, SBUs will report directly to the sector, regardless of whether they are departments, divisions, or groups. As one means of providing opportunities for organizational growth and the development of managers, SBUs can "grow in place"—from department to division to group level—without major restructuring. In the revised planning and management system, the role of the SBU general manager has not significantly changed.

One sector, the International Sector, has a dual role. In addition to managing specific country affiliates, this sector is responsible for the integration of international resources and capabilities in support of other sectors' international strategies. Working with the other sectors and corporate staff components, the International Sector helps assure that individual SBU strategies are consistent with and supportive of the company's worldwide business objectives.

Essentially, the revised management system moves General Electric from strategic *planning* as a process designed for one level (the SBU) to stratetgic *management* as a system for all levels. The major objectives sought are to provide managers with the tools, the channels of communication, and the timely information to cope with the new environment of the 1980s.

MEDIUM-SIZE COMPANIES: EATON CORPORATION

Planning is not new to Eaton. The roots of business planning reach back to Eaton's beginnings when J. O. Eaton, then in New Jersey, selected Cleveland—an early motor capital—as the site of his new axle plant. By the 1940s, rolling forecasts were already in use by the firm. In the years since, the planning process has become more and more involved.

The increasingly complex business environment of this decade has placed a higher priority on precise understanding of the present so that Eaton's businesses may be more accurately directed into the future. Planning has never been a separate activity at Eaton; it has always been interwoven with the general expertise required of managers throughout the world.

The strategic plan for Eaton's businesses is more than a series of projections of past trends and financial schedules. Through it, management analyzes and evaluates the total environment in which the company operates—today and in the future. It includes an assessment of external business factors and internal operating strengths and weaknesses in marketing strategy, pricing, design, quality, manufacturing capacity, and efficiency, as well as in customer and supplier relationships.

The plan includes an analysis of market share and an evaluation of competitors' strengths and weaknesses. This analysis outlines a product's expected life cycle, capital expenditure trends, technological trends, economic conditions, availability of manpower, and even social and political pressures.

Strategic planning is management's tool for controlling and shaping Eaton's businesses to achieve the corporate purpose. Through the self-analysis resulting from strategic planning, management understands today's complex company and environment better than at any time in the company's history. This has led to the setting of more precise objectives and has achieved a unity of direction in attaining those objectives.

Product-Market Segment: Understanding the Basic Unit of Eaton's Businesses

The strategic planning process is organized around the corporation's basic building blocks, called product-market segments of businesses. In all, Eaton has more than 400 product-market segments, many of them closely related. The precise management of a $2 billion company is aided by understanding the detailed nature of these basic units of the corporation.

Product-market segments consist of a single product or a family of related products that go into a well-defined and unified market. Each of these businesses generates its own revenues, operating costs, investments, and strategic action plans. For example, Eaton's engine components operation manufactures and markets engine valves. The engine valve businesses consist of a number of product-market segments including passenger car valves, aircraft valves, and heavy-duty truck valves. Businesses take on geographic limits, too, such as passenger car valves—North America, Europe, Latin America.

In time, Eaton's businesses may be larger or smaller. Some will be discarded, and new ones will be conceived and created within the corporation. Or entirely new businesses may be acquired.

Overall Objectives and Strategies

The Eaton of the 1980s will continue to be a diversified international company, directing its resources around the world to businesses which have potential for a high market share, price leadership, and above-average return on assets employed.

Eaton will build on its balanced skills in engineering, manufacturing, and marketing, with an ongoing emphasis on product leadership attained through increased research, engineering programs, product development, and testing. High value will continue to be placed on an entrepreneurial approach to selected new businesses. Strong emphasis on planning and the vigorous execution of plans will mark Eaton's thrust into the next decade.

Some of Eaton's specific corporate objectives and strategies are as follows:

• Pursue selective business line acquisitions or divestitures to enlarge, redirect, or dispose of existing businesses where internal development alone will not serve return-on-asset or cash-generation objectives.

• Expand Eaton through acquisition of, or merger with, one or more large companies in markets beyond those that are already heavily served by the company.

• Achieve a mix of businesses that would provide increased growth in earnings per share.

• Add businesses that would lessen Eaton's vulnerability to short-term declines in the world economy.

• Establish Eaton's presence in selected new markets.

• Supplement Eaton's professional skills in management, marketing, engineering, and manufacturing.

• Maintain strong supplier relationships to assure a constant flow of purchased materials, permitting capital resources to be concentrated on market expansion and market share improvement.

• Achieve a steady reduction in the assets required to generate sales.

• Increase worldwide exports to adjust to demand peaks and to achieve more sales in developing and less developed countries.

• Achieve increased productivity through innovative employee relations practices that encourage and develop employee involvement.

• Strengthen programs to identify and develop tomorrow's management talent, increasing the depth behind each management position.

• Operate as a concerned, enlightened, and socially responsible corporate citizen of the world community.

• Maintain a dividend payout which, when coupled with stock appreciation, will give shareholders a combined return that exceeds returns on comparable investments.

• Achieve the following corporate operating results:

Pre-tax profit on sales	12.0%
After-tax profit on sales	6.2%
Pre-tax profit on average assets employed	17.0%
After-tax profit on equity	18.5%

These objectives will change as the mix of Eaton's businesses changes because of different market growth rates and investment allocations. They will also change as profitability and risks are modified due to external political and economic forces. A variety of action plans are at work throughout Eaton to achieve these objectives. They range from the action plans at the product-market segment level to broad corporate plans regarding acquisitions, divestitures, capital planning, and risk-taking.

SMALL COMPANIES: NATIONAL DENTAL COMPANY

There are those who think that planning and strategic thinking are luxuries reserved for large firms. On the contrary, strategic thinking is just as important in smaller businesses as it is in large companies. An example that we have made up here is the "National" Dental Company, a fictitious $120 million dental distribution company based on a real firm in the industry. Because our previous examples have been public companies with varying degrees of visibility, a description of those businesses was not required. In the case of National, however, we feel that some background information will be beneficial.

National Dental Company is a direct-sales distribution organization concentrating on the selling and distribution of supplies and equipment to the dental community (composed of dentists, dental laboratories, and institutions). At present, there are over 60 branch offices and five distribution centers, employing approximately 335 salespeople altogether. Each territory salesperson services about 150 accounts.

There are several major dealer organizations that serve the U.S. dental community in direct competition with National. At present, National is thought to be the second largest (in terms of sales volume) with approximately 10 percent of the total U.S. market. In addition, there is competition from local and regional supply networks. It is thought that the major chains (National, Healthco, Codesco, Patterson, S.S. White, and Saslow) currently account for close to 45 percent of the total domestic dental business, whereas local competitors have 20 percent of the business. The remaining 35 percent is served by other distribution channels—mail order houses and direct sales by manufacturers.

The entire domestic dental market is composed of an estimated 105,000 practicing dentists and 10,000 dental laboratories, as well as dental colleges and government institutions. In 1977, the total retail market was believed to range from $900 million to $1 billion, with the practicing dentist segment accounting for 80 percent of this volume. Total volume has experienced a 10 percent annual growth rate since 1971, and is expected to approximate this level through 1982. Factors that affect market growth include:

Individual educational level, which determines health consciousness
Discretionary income
Third-party and prepaid dental plans
Population growth

Approximately 83 percent of the dentists in the United States are solo practitioners. In recent years, however, dentist productivity has increased due to implementation of "the expanded duties concept." Under this concept, the dentist utilizes the talents of auxiliary individuals—such as technicians, dental assistants, and hygienists—along with better designed and more productive equipment.

National approaches this marketplace through the use of its salespeople and specialists. The company attempts to establish long-term customer relationships by emphasizing quality of service and knowledgeability of sales personnel. The National representative strives to be considered a member of the practitioner's dental team. This is accomplished by informing the dental practitioner of new products and techniques; by promptly attending to his equipment repair needs; and by making certain that his supply needs are fulfilled. Supply is handled through a Materials Control System program in which National institutes an automatic inventory control procedure for the dentist's supplies.

Another route used to contact purchasers of dental products is through dental association conventions and exhibits. These shows serve a dual purpose: first, to ensure that the dental practitioner's knowledge of the state of the art remains current; and second, to introduce new equipment and supplies, and to encourage the practitioner's use of these. Most state dental societies and several local societies conduct annual meetings at which National displays in the areas it serves. In addition, National displays at the annual session of the American Dental Association.

A third method that National uses is local information clinics on dental technology held in conjunction with, and with the support of, manufacturers. These clinics, which are usually conducted in branch offices, serve a purpose similar to that of the exhibits, but the clinics specialize in specific problem areas and special aspects of dental technology.

The focus of National's selling effort, and thus its entire business thrust, is geared to helping the dentist increase his production, which increases his demand for the products and services that National provides. The goal is to become the dentist's consultant, helping him achieve financial success, the end result of which is National's own growth and success.

With this as background information, let us now review the company's strategic planning process. The first step was to establish a business charter as a framework under which the company operates.

National's Business Charter

The purpose of the National Dental Company is to engage in business activities that improve the quality of health care provided to consumers on a worldwide basis. This will be accomplished through creating a selectively positioned health care company with a balanced blend of distribution, manufacturing, and service business in various related and integrated industries established principally in the more developed marketplaces of the world.

The primary objective for National is to build outward from dental distribution capabilities and expand in selected markets. Through selective expansion encompassing forward, backward, and horizontal integration, an attempt will be made to build National into a leadership position in the total dental marketplace. The end result will be an integrated company that exhibits above-average growth with consistent and stable earnings.

After management determined in which direction it wanted to move, its next step was to understand the market. National was divided into two distinct business units: Distribution and Financial Services. Because of its small size and its limited resources, National employed consultants to help do the job.

Dental Market

The analysis of data on the dental industry indicates that the dental market has had a historical sales growth rate (since 1970) of 10–12 percent per year, and is projected to have a future annual growth rate of 9–11 percent. In terms of real growth rates, the former (historical) is equivalent to 4–5 percent, and the latter (projected) is equivalent to 5–6 percent. Some key estimates and data are summarized in Table 8.

Lastly, it is worth noting that the dental sundries category (especially endodontic and orthodontic products) has exhibited, and will continue to exhibit, above-average growth. Teeth and gold, on the other hand, are expected to exhibit below-average growth. The underlying cause for this growth-rate behavior has

Table 8. Estimated and projected sales of dental industry.

Source	Estimated 1975 Manufacturers' Sales	Historical Compounded Growth Rate (Real)	Projected Growth Rate (Real)
Arthur D, Little, Inc.	$450 million	4–5%	5–6%
Becker Securities Corp.	$460 million	4%	5–7%
American Dental Trade Association	$445 million	4–5%	Not available
Citibank	$440 million	3–5%	5–7%

been the greater emphasis on caries prevention and tooth-structure preservation.

There seems to have been a slight acceleration in annual growth rate in recent years as a result of larger graduation classes from dental schools and a growing number of people visiting their dentists on a regular or intermittent basis.

External Environment of the Company

• Population coverage by private third-party insurance plans will continue to increase, reaching the 82 million level by 1985 from the current 1980 level of 60 million.

• Two of the key factors that underpin the growth of the dental market—namely, the number of dentists and patient visits—will continue to grow at least at the same rate as they have in the past: approximately 2 percent per year for each.

• There will be a continuation of recent trends toward consolidation, at both the dentist and the dealer level. Currently, 82 percent of all dentists are "solo" practitioners; the historical trend will reduce that percentage to 75 percent by 1982.

• There will be no further increase in penetration of the dental sundries market by mail order operations. Present estimates suggest that the mail order channel represents about 25 percent of all sundries purchased by the general practitioner.

• Antitrust activity by the U.S. government against the American Dental Association will have a limited effect on the individual dental practitioner's practice of dentistry. As a result, any actions should not be detrimental to the dental business.

• During the next five years, some form of national health care legislation will probably be enacted. This legislation will cause demand for health care to continue its above-average growth rate.

• Above-average profitability will remain available in the specialty health care area, and government legislation that restricts profits severely will not be enacted.

• Real growth in the Gross National Product from 1980 through 1985 will average 3.6 percent annually. At some point during the five-year period, an economic contraction will occur, which is expected to affect National adversely.

Figure 20. A competitive grid showing National's position in the industry.

Industry/Products Maturity

	Embryonic	Growth	Mature	Aging
Dominant				
Strong		National		
Favorable				
Tenable				
Weak				
Nonviable				

Competitive Position

Having taken all of these factors into consideration, the company's top management developed competitive grids (see Figure 20), then a complete competitor analysis covering:

Market strength
Distribution
Financial characteristics
Management capabilities
Customer service
Pricing
Vendor leverage
Private-label programs

When all of this analysis was completed, senior management then formulated its target objectives.

National Dental Company: Statement of Objectives

1. Immediate emphasis will be placed on implementation of action programs which continue the reversal of the recent performance of the distribution business. These programs will center on:
   Motivation of sales personnel and branch managers
   Upgrading of the central marketing effort
   Upgrading of the operational effort
   Centralization of purchasing for effectiveness and cost reduction
2. Through a combination of internal growth and acquisition, achieve market leadership (in terms of share) by 1981.
3. Establish National Dental Company as the most profitable major chain in the retail dental industry.
4. Maintain stability and growth in earnings, and provide an adequate return on invested assets.
5. Strengthen the central National support staff to enhance capabilities in the areas of product management, marketing re-

search, market development, purchasing, and personnel and sales management.

6. After significant improvements have been made in the present business, expand the marketing network to establish some form of representation which will afford coverage of all major markets in the United States.

7. Determine business areas in which operating efficiencies can occur, and then implement action programs to facilitate their occurrence.

(Of course, as part of the plan, specific and numerical targets were identified, but we have not included them.)

Operating plans for distinct business units were developed, covering both the long and short term. In addition, because of the volatility of the U.S. economy, which greatly affects the business (particularly interest rates, layoffs, and softening of contract benefits awarded in labor negotiations), contingency plans were developed.

We hope that this brief example shows the applicability of strategic planning to smaller businesses. Size is not the critical factor as to whether or not strategic planning can be utilized—survival is.

5

LOOKING AHEAD:
Thinking Globally,
Acting Locally

The era when we were a strong technological giant is over.
　　　　　—PAUL F. CHENCA
　　　　　V.P., General Motors Research Laboratories

Every decade puts its mark on our industrial environment. The quiet 1950s, the growth-oriented 1960s, the crisis-ridden 1970s—each had its own unique quality. The 1980s will be no different. Of course, the decade will build upon trends started in earlier decades and on the emergence of new ones, but its character will be shaped mostly by a conservatism fed by fears of inflation, energy shortages, rumors of war, and other crises.

Perhaps never before has the western world looked ahead to a new decade with more uncertainty. Emerging from the 1970s is a world aware of limits on its natural resources; of rising international tensions and a decline in global security; and of its failure, thus far, to solve the worries of inflation and energy shortages, let alone social conflicts around the globe. However, it is our opinion that the Unites States stands at the threshold of a new era. Perhaps never before has industry faced so many problems at one time, while holding such promise for the future.

We believe that planning must and will, by the rapid changes of events, play a more vital role in the development and generation of business in the 1980s. In the corporate hierarchy, there is no group better equipped to analyze, monitor, assess, and give needed advice in formulating goals and objectives than the strategic planning group. Planning brings to the party all the basic tools senior executives need to plan the growth of their businesses: industrial market research, acquisition analysis, economics, financial planning, venture analysis, modeling, technology assessment, and manpower planning. As environmental complexities and uncertainties increase business risks, executives at all levels will depend more than ever before on formal planning.

LIFE IN THE 1980s

Let's look at some of the social and economic trends which are already making themselves visible and which planners in both government and private industry are watching carefully. What follows should shed some light on the kind of business environment we can expect to find in this decade. Managers should monitor these trends and keep informed of their consequences.

We're Growing Older

The most obvious change in our society is simply that we are growing older. In 1970, the median age was just under 28. By the turn of the century, it will hit 35. Over the next 15 years, the most rapidly increasing segment of the population will be the 25- to 44-year-old age group (see Table 9). On the whole, of course, this is the most employable and productive age group in the U.S. labor

Table 9. The U.S. population is getting older.

Age Group (in years)	Population (in millions of people)		Percentage Increase 1977–1990
	1977	1990	
Under 18	64.2	64.8	1%
18–24	28.6	25.1	(12%)
25–44	56.7	77.7	37%
45–54	23.4	25.3	8%
55 and over	43.8	50.6	16%
Total population	216.7	243.5	12%

SOURCE: U.S. Dept. of Commerce

force. It is also the group with the highest spending profile. Its numbers will jump by 37 percent to 78 million in 1990 from 58 million today. After 1990, however, the 25- to 34-year-old group will top out and will decline throughout the 1990s.

As a result of the shift, the U.S. economy must create jobs and incomes for a rapidly expanding, mature labor force. After that, it must adjust to a slower rate of growth. The most immediate problem, and the problem of the early 1980s, is to produce ten million new jobs.

In view of this, how do things look for the 1980s? It will be a decade of enormous opportunities for growth, as well as of severe strain on the economy. In the early 1980s, pressure will build for expanded employment programs. But by 1985, with an older and more slowly expanding labor force, growth will come harder.

Families Are Changing

The movement toward single-parent and individual households is well entrenched and should continue to grow. As a people, we will continue to experience high divorce rates and deferred childbearing, although marriages and remarriages will remain in vogue.

Table 10. Changes in consumer characteristics, 1980–1990.

	1980	1990
Total labor force (millions)	97	113
Labor force, 16 years and over		
Men working	77%	77%
Women working	47%	50%
Divorce and marriage (millions per year)		
Divorce	1.1	N/A
Marriage	2.1	N/A
Education attained (25 years and over)		
High school graduate	38%	39%
Attended or graduated college	28%	31%
Number of households (millions)	80	89
One- and two-person households (percentage)	53%	57%
Household income (in current dollars; percent distribution)		
$15,000–$24,999	28%	26%
$25,000 and over	23%	33%

SOURCE: U.S. Dept. of Commerce

Inflation will be somewhat offset by two-wage-earner households. The new consumers may feel poorer, but they will be better off in real terms. With fewer children and more two-wage-earner households, discretionary income will rise. So, by the mid-1980s, we will be better educated, older, more prosperous, with fewer children, and likely to be remarried (see Table 10).

Sun Belt Migration to Slow, and Flight from the Cities to Continue

The aging of Americans should help dampen the population move to the Sun Belt. Since the young are prone to migrate, the movement's tempo should slow somewhat, particularly if the trend toward two-wage-earner households continues. However, the Sun Belt should experience a boom after the year 2000, when large numbers of retirees will move to warmer surroundings.

Table 11. Flight to suburbs and small towns (in millions of people).

Type of Area	1980	1990
Central cities	59.4	55.3
Suburbs	88.0	102.9
Non-metropolitan areas	72.9	83.3

SOURCE: U.S. Dept. of Commerce

Does this imply that the central cities will undergo a revival through the return of the middle class? Although some neighborhoods in some cities have come alive, planners would be rash to regard these isolated success stories as the forerunners of a "back to the cities" movement. Substantial urban resettlement occurs only where the urban economy offers high-paying, white collar jobs. Most central cities will continue to deteriorate because they do not possess the kind of economic base that would cause a "back to the cities" movement. The more likely trends are shown in Table 11.

Marketing Concerns

The increasing level of education for Americans will have major implications for marketing. A more sophisticated consuming public will be highly conscious of the durability, functionality, repairability, quality of design, and overall value of the goods it buys. A large segment of this group also will be likely to focus on such issues as packaging materials, the contents of product labeling, the clarity of instructions on the use and care of products, and the warranties that back them up.

This generation, particularly among the college-educated, is much more environmentally conscious. Although there may be less social activism than there was in the Sixties, concern for the environment and consciousness of future resource shortages will carry over into consumption behavior patterns. Products with recyclable packaging will be preferred. Appliances will be chosen on the basis of their energy efficiency and repairability. Durability and gas mileage will be important considerations in choosing a car.

End of the Youth Culture

The postwar "baby boom" generation has had a tremendous impact on the national scene. In the Sixties, as this generation passed through its adolescence and college years, we saw the flowering of the youth culture. The Eighties will see the end of the youth culture, as the adolescent and college age population declines in absolute numbers. In the early 1980s, the American ideal of onward and upward, ever higher pay and ever more responsibility, will have to change for a while as energy shortages and lowered expectations become a way of life.

It is also becoming clearer that schooling will not necessarily repay the investment put into it. For this reason, enrollments will continue to decline (see Table 12), and dropouts will increase until the late 1980s, after which these trends will start to reverse themselves. Hence, during the early 1980s, we shall see less and less pressure for additional educational spending and taxes.

In the 1980s, as many as four out of every ten college students will be over 25 years old, many of them part-timers already embarked on careers. Retirees and other adults will attend noncollegiate training programs designed for self-improvement. Public education will be asked to serve increasingly specialized groups.

Table 12. Projected school enrollments (in millions of students).

School Level	1980	1988	Projected Percent Increase
Preschool (ages 3–4)	2.0	2.6	28%
Elementary	29.8	33.9	14%
High school	14.3	11.9	(17%)
College	12.4	11.0	(11%)

More Outside Services Needed

As a result of the increasing number of working wives, more outside services will be required to replace some of the homemaker's traditional chores. Child care facilities will be needed for preschool-aged children. Schools may have to extend their services to provide after-hours supervision for the children of working parents.

In addition to outside services, products that aid the working wife will be in great demand. With a majority of women working during the next decade, some shifts in shopping habits will occur, especially for staple items and routine purchases. More shopping will be conducted by telephone and will use mass media communication techniques such as television, radio, and newspapers, with delivery or pickup at a later time. Increased use of mail order, catalog stores, and video-disc shopping is also likely.

Greater Market Segmentation and Specialty Retailing

As a result of more diverse life styles, greater market segmentation and more specialty retailing are expected in the future. For instance, the same working wife and mother who may be a consumer of convenience foods during the working week may cook a gourmet dinner from scratch on the weekend. And consider this: will Ronald McDonald (the Emmet Kelly of the 1970s) be sufficiently dignified for an aging clientele? Remember, by 1990, John Travolta will be 35. Specialty retailing is in step with the widening range of future consumer interests, activities, affluence, and the growing need for self-expression.

One aspect of the greater individualism of the postwar generation is the need for the expression of personal creativity. Home ownership provides a major outlet for handicrafts, do-it-yourself projects, gourmet cooking, and various other artistic endeavors. The current eclecticism in home decoration is the result of a desire for home decor to be an expression of personal taste. Other areas include travel, recreation, canning, weaving, wine making, and bread baking. This trend is really a variation on the theme of individualism and "doing your own thing." Even though there will be a greater concern over technology and its benefits (and its potential harm) to mankind, consumers will still search for technological novelty. Current manifestations are seen in video recorders, electronic games, computerized chess, and programmable calculators.

The adult population is also manifesting a strong interest in outdoor activities of all types, which allow the participants to "get back to nature," and sports, which promote physical fitness. A much larger number of people are concerned with maintaining healthy bodies through exercise and proper eating habits. This trend has given rise to increased attention to the nutritional content of food and to the concern about the presence of various chemical additives in food.

This interest in a healthy diet is resulting in changing food consumption patterns, which should continue in the future. People are cutting back on their consumption of red meat and other food products high in animal fat or cholesterol. Consumption of fish, poultry, fruits, and vegetables is increasing.

Look to European Trends

Over the past 20 years soothsayers, forecasters, economists, and government prognosticators have gone to California to get a peek at the future. This was fine in the decades of the 1950s and 1960s, but we are convinced that the place to look now is *not* California: California is fine for social and political activism but not for lifestyle trends; the place to look to our future is Europe. Europe has been confronting changing life style patterns with few energy resources, high consumer aspirations, and erratic growth for years, something the United States is just beginning to understand.

For example, even with an abundance of coal, countries such as

West Germany and France have decided to go nuclear. So, regardless of the Three Mile Island incident, the United States will go nuclear, or be kicked into the nuclear age, whether it likes it or not. That will be a major source of electricity in the 1980s and 1990s.

We also should see more electric cars, but these cars will not dominate the market; they will be used for short distances, such as shopping and getting around the neighborhood. The gasoline engine is here to stay for at least the next two decades. Europeans tend to keep their cars longer and to expect durability and good gas mileage. What they expect, Americans are coming to realize. Not surprisingly, since 1970 Americans have started to demand better performance from their automobiles (see Table 13).

Cars are more functional in Europe. They do not play the macho role they have played here in the United States. That doesn't mean to say that they don't play some part in soothing a person's ego. But, because of the expense in operating and owning

Table 13. Some auto industry trends since 1965.

Key Indicator	1965	1970	1977	Percentage of Growth, 1965–1977
Average age of cars in use (years)	5.9	5.6	6.3	6.8%
Tires, passenger cars (in millions)				
Original equipment	51.4	37.5	55.8	8.6%
Replacement	44.9	129.6	129.5	36.8%
Percentage of women among total drivers	40.8%	43.2%	45.7%	13.0%
Sales, new passenger cars (in millions)				
Domestic[1]	8.8	7.1	9.1	3.4%
Imports[2]	0.6	1.3	2.1	250.0%
Total	9.4	8.4	11.2	20.4%
Replacement automobile batteries (in millions)	29.5	27.9	54.6	85.1%

[1] Includes domestic models produced in Canada.
[2] Excludes domestic models produced in Canada.
SOURCE: U.S. Department of Commerce

a car, people will look to other forms or outlets in expressing their individuality.

It is not by chance that the high-fashion disco-oriented stores are in vogue in the United States. It would have been easy for planners to predict this if they had visited Europe a decade ago. Years ago, young English men and women turned to fashion to express or to highlight individual differences, because cars and houses were beyond the reach of most of them, at least when they were in their twenties and early thirties. Ten years later in the United States, we see white suits, slit skirts, disco-related fashions, every imaginable piece of material draping the human body. Why? Because it's hard to express your individuality when you buy a small boxy car that has four seats and a stick shift, and gives you 30 to 40 miles per gallon.

With gasoline prices rising, we will think differently about driving long distances. This doesn't mean that recreation or travel will diminish, but small cars are too uncomfortable for long distances. Air travel will increase, and the rental car industry will experience good steady growth.

In fact, the recent deregulation of airline fares provides impetus for this thinking. Transatlantic charters have already shown that a great number of travelers are willing to endure Spartan treatment in exchange for substantial savings. We should see a new generation of jet planes going into service in the 1980s, and airlines will try to cut the time spent on long walks in terminals and in waiting for baggage.

NEGATIVE TRENDS

Labor Shortages

Planners should pay just as much attention to the less than positive trends and counter trends affecting our industrial environment. For example, in the early 1980s, the problem for economic policy-makers will be to provide jobs. This will reverse by the late 1980s, and labor shortages will develop. This phenomenon will play havoc with personnel managers who rely on vast quantities of cheap labor.

As a practical matter, entry-level workers will be supplied from Mexico. Mexico has a high birth rate and a relatively young population, and lacks the capacity to create jobs fast enough to absorb all those who seek work. At present, there are probably 10 million Mexicans in the United States illegally. Mexico will soon be using its vast oil reserves to pressure the U.S. to take more of them. By the end of the decade, we will welcome this influx of new workers. By the end of the century, more than a quarter of the U.S. population will speak Spanish as a primary language.

Some time after the year 2000, the U.S. will face the critical question of how a stable labor force can sustain an increasing number of retirees and their dependents. Furthermore, unionization should decline in the 1990s because management policies will be directed to keeping employees content and happy in their jobs. During the late 1980s, business will experience a series of events not dissimilar to those that occurred in the late 1960s. Because of labor shortages, job hopping by bright young managers should increase. This doesn't mean that there will be an over-abundance of senior level positions. On the contrary, because of slower growth, there will be certain businesses, such as retailing, where store managers, finding their careers slowing down in midstream, will become susceptible to executive unionization.

Solidifying of Class Structure and Growing Social Disruptions

In addition to all this, the U.S. will experience a new phenomenon, a solidifying of class structure. Since about the late 1960s, a second income has become almost essential if a family expects to buy a home and enjoy some of the discretionary extras in life. In the 1979

Harris Perspective Service study, the majority of Americans viewed health insurance, a telephone, a car, life insurance, a savings account, a house, and a yearly vacation as necessities. Can these desires be met by a one-wage-earner household? The two-wage-earner household, almost by itself, threatens to widen our class differences.

Moreover, there is a new element not to be overlooked—the disadvantaged. We are in danger of creating a permanent group of marginal workers whose lack of skills will keep them chronically unemployed, even in the face of a shortage of unskilled workers, just when our social consciousness will be at an all-time low. This could cause severe social disruptions in the next two decades.

Science on the Wane

Many leaders in industry, science, and government are deeply concerned that we are losing momentum in our technological effort. Throughout most of our history, we have expanded knowl-

Table 14. Sluggish investment of seed money, 1968–1978 (in millions of 1972 dollars).*

	1968	1978	Change	Percentage Change
Total R&D	29,798	31,136	+1,338	+4%
Federal government	18,077	15,678	−2,399	−13
Industry	10,906	14,338	+3,432	+31
Basic research	3,965	3,980	+15	0
Federal government	2,802	2,758	−44	−2
Industry	648	589	−59	−9
Applied research	6,252	7,061	+809	+13
Federal government	3,441	3,479	+38	+1
Industry	2,574	3,193	+619	+24
Development	19,581	20,095	+514	+3
Federal government	11,835	9,440	−2,395	−20
Industry	7,684	10,556	+2,872	+37

* Totals include funding by universities and other institutions.
SOURCE: National Science Foundation.

Table 15. Interest in science wanes in schools.

	1960	1976
Engineering degrees as percentage of total degrees earned	10	5
Percentage of students taking one science course—grades 7 to 10	64	49
Percentage of high school students beyond grade 10 taking no science courses	N/A	50

SOURCE: National Institute of Education

edge and selected new options to fashion progress. Perry Pascarella, executive editor of *Industry Week,* has remarked, "Seed money for technological innovation—research and spending—has not kept pace with inflation since hitting a peak in the late Sixties." Under pressure to maintain profits in the face of rising costs, businesses and government have reduced their R&D budgets in real terms (see Table 14).

In addition, Scholastic Aptitude Test (SAT) scores have been steadily declining over the last decade, and fewer people are studying science or engineering (see Table 15). Does this imply that the pool of highly trained young engineering graduates will diminish just when we need them the most? Citizens unacquainted with the tools used by scientists must rely on blind instinct or the opinion of experts. This turns such experts into an elite class. As Plato suggested, a democracy cannot work without educated people.

No Homogeneous Consumer

It is evident from the data that consumers' tastes, desires, and needs are changing. The 1980s will see no homogeneous "typical" consumer. Markets will appeal to different people at different times. Sometimes things will seem incongruous, but this is to be expected. Consumers will make trade-offs between utility and quality. They will question technological advancement, even while demanding exotic devices to satisfy their personal needs.

As we move into a "me-" rather than a "we"-oriented society, business opportunities exist at all levels. It is not by chance that "The Limited" and "Petrie's" fashion stores are popular and that children's cereals and TV programs are under attack. This is just a manifestation of what is happening throughout the society.

The next two decades will see household formations on an unprecedented scale. (By household, we mean any place where one or more persons reside.) Self-expression and self-fulfillment will become the order of the day. Personal technology and household aids will experience extraordinary growth. And finally, the concern for health and nutrition will entrench itself in our daily habits. This isn't to say that we won't eat hamburgers and candy bars or drink soda, but that we will worry about it more.

Age of Uncertainty

Motherhood no longer is an automatic goal of a young woman. God and country no longer involve universally accepted values. Confidence in business, schools, unions, government, and other institutions is waning. It is an age of uncertainty.

We know of no way to meet the challenges of the future other than by studying your customer's present and future needs. The market has changed and will continue to change, and only the smart, well-informed business manager can take advantage of these trends.

We hope that we have demonstrated the need for good strategic planning. But, even after you have adopted a planning system, it is wise to remember that this is only the beginning. Good intelligence is merely the first step; analysis of the implications of the data and how it relates to your business is crucial. Planning is not an academic exercise—it means survival itself.

Bibliography

Allen, Michael G. "Diagramming GE's Planning for What's Watt." *Planning Review,* September 1977.

Allen, Wayne M. "A Theory on the Cause of Cost Growth." *Procurement Association,* August 1963.

Berg, Norman. "Strategic Planning for Conglomerate Companies." *Harvard Business Review, May–June 1965.*

Blass, Walter. "Economic Planning, European Style." *Harvard Business Review,* September–October 1963.

Branch, Melville C. *The Corporate Planning Process.* New York: American Management Association, 1962.

Conrad, Gordon R. "Unexplored Assets for Diversification." *Harvard Business Review,* September–October 1963.

Cordiner, Ralph J. *New Frontiers for Professional Managers.* New York: McGraw-Hill, 1956.

Drucker, Peter F. *Managing for Results.* New York: Harper & Row, 1964.

————. *The Practice of Management.* New York: Harper & Row, 1954.

Durant, Will. *Caesar and Christ.* New York: Simon & Schuster, 1944.

Ellis, Darryl J., and Pekar, Peter P., Jr. "Project Assessment: A Guide for Implementation." *Project Management Quarterly,* September 1977.

————. "Linking Resources to Strategic Marketing Plans." *Industrial Marketing Management,* 6:1 (1977).

————. "Tracking Venture Strategy." *Planning Review,* May 1977.

Fair, Charles. *From the Jaws of Victory.* New York: Simon & Schuster, 1971.

Ginzberg, Eli. *Effecting Change in Large Organizations.* New York: Columbia University Press, 1957.

Golde, Roger A. "Practical Planning for Small Business." *Harvard Business Review,* October–November 1964.

Granger, Charles H. "The Best-Laid. . . ." *The Controller,* August 1962.

———. "The Hierarchy of Objectives." *Harvard Business Review,* May–June 1964.

Hardy, James M. *Corporate Planning for Nonprofit Organizations.* New York: Association Press, 1972.

Julien, Claude. *America's Empire.* New York: Pantheon, 1971.

Kami, Michael J. "Planning and Planners in the Age of Discontinuity." *Planning Review,* March 1976.

Kitchell, Raymond E. *A Summary of Current Planning Concepts.* Washington, D.C.: U.S. Bureau of the Budget, 1962.

Kloman, Erasmus H. *Unmanned Space Project Management.* Washington, D.C.: National Aeronautics and Space Administration, NASA SP-4901, 1972.

Kotler, Philip. *Market Management.* Englewood Cliffs, N.J.: Prentice-Hall, 1972.

Lebreton, Preston, and Henning, Dale A. *Planning Theory.* Englewood Cliffs, N.J.: Prentice-Hall, 1961.

Levitt, Theodore. "Marketing Myopia." *Harvard Business Review,* July–August 1960.

Lucas, Arthur, and Livingston, William G. *Long-Range Planning—The Capital Appropriations Program.* AMA Management Report No. 44. New York: American Management Association, 1960.

Mace, Myles T. "The President and Corporate Planning." *Harvard Business Review,* January–February 1965.

Newman, William H., and Logan, James P. *Management of Expanding Enterprises.* New York: Columbia University Press, 1955.

Pekar, Peter P., Jr. "Matching Action Plans to Market Development Stage." *Planning Review,* July–August 1976.

———. "Looking into the 1980's." *Aftermarket Executive,* August–September 1979.

———. "Planning: A Guide to Implementation." *Managerial Planning,* July–August 1980.

———, and Burack, Elmer H. "New Directions in Manpower Planning and Control." *Managerial Planning,* July–August 1977.

Rosen, Stephen. *Future Facts.* New York: Simon & Schuster, 1976.

Index

A&P Co., 15–16
Abercrombie & Fitch, 55
action plans, 61, 70, 82–83
age, median, in U.S., 134–135
AMC, 56
Armed Services Procurement
    Regulations, 80
automotive industry, 20–21, 56,
    121–125
    in future, 141–142

Barbarossa, Frederick, 7
Boston Consulting Group, 48, 50
Bowmar Instrument Company,
    38–39
budgeting, 10
business areas, distinct, 34–36
    at Eaton Corp., 122–123
    at GE, 108–109
    profile of, 41–43
businesses, differences in, related
    to type, 12–13

cancer, research for, 1–2
Carroll, Daniel T., 63–64
Casey, Samuel B., Jr., interview
    with, 92–97
cash cows, 48
Catholic Church, 6–8
chief executive officer (CEO),
    planning by, 24–25

Chrysler Corporation, 56
class structure, 143–144
Coca-Cola, 52
communication, 12–13
compensation, incentive, 118–119
competition, internal, at IBM,
    99–100
competitive position, determin-
    ing, 39
    distinct business area profile
        in, 41–43
    industry profile in, 40–41
    matrix analysis for, 44, 48–49,
        50
    worksheet for, 45–47
computer industry, 98–107
Constantine, Emperor, 6
consumer characteristics, changes
    in, 134–146
contraction expenditures, 73
contracts, government, 77–81
    close-out of, 81–82
control, 101
    management, 103
    operational, 103
corporate planning, see planning
cost accounting standards, 79–80
Cost Schedule Control Systems Criteria
    Joint Implementation Guide
    (Defense Dept.), 80
Crusades, 7

"crystal ball" syndrome, 26
"cure-all" syndrome, 26–27

Defense, Dept. of, U.S., 80
dental products industry,
    125–132
"dogs," 48

Eaton Corporation, 121–125
electronics industry, consumer, 20
environment, 49–50
    forecasting and, 50–53
Europe, trends from, 140–142

families in U.S., 135–136
financial planning, 76
    expenditures in, 72–73
    tables for, 74–75
food industry, retail
    market planning in, 70–72
    planning by, 15–16
Ford, Henry, 6
Ford Motor Co., 21, 56
forecasting, 32, 50–53
future-position determination
    54–56
F. W. Woolworth, 22

Gardner, John W., 10
General Dynamics, 81
General Electric Company, 34,
    36, 54–55, 63
    planning at, 107–114, 117–121
General Motors, 20–21, 56
GNP growth rate, 36
goals, 82–83, 94–95
    defined, 57–58, 60–61
    statements of, 58–60
Gould, Inc., 63–64
Grant Co., 22
Great Atlantic & Pacific Tea Co.,
    Inc. (A&P), 15–16
growth industries, 36–38

Hero of Alexandria, 5
Hurley Laboratory, 100

IBM, 98–107
implementation of planning,
    time horizon for, 28
incentive compensation, 118–119
income, per capita personal, 17
industry profile, 40–41
information sources, 84–90
innovation
    time cycle for, 3
    technological, 144–145
investment management,
    116–118

Japan, planning in, 18–20
Jefferson, Thomas, 9

Kloman, Erasmus H., 78
K Mart, 17, 21–22
Kobayshi, Yotaro, 18
Kresge Company (K Mart), 17,
    21–22

labor shortage in future, 142–143
Lockheed Aircraft Corporation,
    59–60
long-term planning
    case-studies of, 20–22
    changes affecting, 29
Luther, Martin, 7

maintenance expenditures, 73
management
    control, 101, 103
    levels of, planning by, 24
Marco, Dale H., 22
marketing, in future, 137–138
market planning, 70–72
market strength, see competitive
    position
Martin Marietta Corp., 67–69

matrix analysis of competitive position, 44, 48–49, 50
medical supply industry, 36, 125–132
Mexico, 143
Model T Ford, 6
Monroe, James, 9
multiunit business, 32
  business areas of, defining, 34–36
  Pullman, Inc. as, 92–97

NASA, 66–69
National Dental Company (pseud.), 125–132
National Planning Commission, 28
Navy, U.S., 81
new ventures expenditures, 73
Nixon, Richard M., 1

objectives, 57–58
  see also goals
operating plans, 66
operational control, 101, 103
Ozeki, Toshio, 18

Pascarella, Perry, 145
Penn Central Railroad, 15, 92
Pennington, Malcolm W., 57–58, 60–61
per capita disposable personal income, 17
performance measurement requirements, 80
"Persian messenger" syndrome, 27
personal income, per capita, 17
planning
  benefits of, 23
  by the Church, 6–8
  by Eaton Corporation, 121–125

formal, questions to ask in, 33
  at GE, see General Electric Company
  by IBM, 98–107
  implementation of, time horizon for, 28
  information sources for, 84–90
  for long-term, see long-term planning
  personnel for, see planning staff
  pitfalls of, 26–27
  in Roman Empire, 5–6
  short-range, 29
  by small companies, 125–132
  time devoted to, 24, 93
  in U.S., history of, 8–10
  see also planning process
planning process, 32–34
  action plans in, 61
  competitive position in, 39–50
  completion of, 82–83
  distinct business areas and, 34–36
  financial planning in, 72–76
  forecasting in, 50–53
  future-position determination in, 54–56
  goal-setting in, 57–61, 94–95
  information sources for, 84–90
  market planning in, 70–72
  operating plans in, 66–70
  product life cycle determination in, 36–39
  at Pullman, Inc., 94–97
  strategies in, 62–66
Planning Review (magazine), 57–58
planning staf, 24–26, 97
  characteristics of, 10–11
  at GE, 119–121
  at IBM, 104
plant nutrient industry, 35, 36
product life cycle, 36–39

product-market segment, *see* business areas, distinct
profit, concentration on, 14
Pullman, Inc., 92–97

railroads, 9, 55–56
  planning by, 15
replacement expenditures, 73
retail industry, 21–22
risk, strategic, 12–13
Roman Empire, 5–6

screens, business, 111–114 *passim*
Sears, Roebuck and Co., 16–17
Seward, William, 9
shoe industry, 43
short-range planning, 29
Sloan, Alfred, 21
soft drink industry, 52
Sony, 20
source list, 84–90
S. S. Kresge Company (K Mart), 17, 21–22
"stars," 48
statement of goals, 58–59
  of Lockheed, 59–60
strategic business unit, *see* business areas, distinct
strategic thinking, *see* planning
strategies, 62, 70
  evaluation of, 64–66
  identification of, 62–64

technological innovation, 144–145

Texas Instruments, 38–39
time horizons
  establishing, 27–29
  for implementation of planning, 28
  for innovation, 3

United States
  affluence in, 17
  age median in, 134–135
  class structure of, 143–144
  contracts from, 77–82
  demographics of, 136–137
  families in, 135–136
  Japanese industry and, 19
  labor shortage in, 142–143
  lifestyle in, changes in, 134–146
  planning in, 8–10
  space program of, 66–69
  youth culture in, 138
"Unmanned Space Project Management" (Kloman), 78
Urban II, Pope, 7

Weinberg, Robert, 62
Wells, H. G., 1
Williams, Grant E., 81–82
Woodside, William S., 27
Woolworth, 22
World Trade Corp., 100
W. T. Grant, 22

youth culture, 138